Mathematizing Student Thinking

Connecting problem solving
to everyday life and building capable
and confident math learners

David Costello

Pembroke Publishers Limited

© 2022 Pembroke Publishers
538 Hood Road
Markham, Ontario, Canada L3R 3K9
www.pembrokepublishers.com

Library and Archives Canada Cataloguing in Publication
Title: Mathematizing student thinking : connecting problem solving to everyday life and building capable and confident math learners / David Costello.
Names: Costello, David (Professional learning facilitator), author.
Identifiers: Canadiana (print) 20210394382 | Canadiana (ebook) 20210394455 | ISBN 9781551383569 (softcover) | ISBN 9781551389561 (PDF)
Subjects: LCSH: Mathematics—Study and teaching (Elementary) | LCSH: Problem solving—Study and teaching (Elementary) | LCSH: Critical thinking—Study and teaching (Elementary)
Classification: LCC QA135.6 .C66 2022 | DDC 372.7—dc23

Editor: Sandy Matos
Cover Design: John Zehethofer
Typesetting: Jay Tee Graphics Ltd.

Printed and bound in Canada
9 8 7 6 5 4 3 2 1

Contents

Introduction

What do we want our students to know about mathematics? While this may seem like a simple question, the answer is not as easy as one might think. Educators want students to be able to see the beauty of mathematics and apply it to their experiences. Students should know that mathematics has a larger purpose. It involves critical thinking and not simply following linear steps to get to the answer. We want students to be creative, flexible, independent **critical thinkers** who can communicate their thoughts, both when they understand and struggle to solve a problem. We want our students to be problem solvers.

Students' Dependence on Their Teachers

Too often, students appear to be going through the motions. Students will work through a problem but cannot properly communicate if they understand or have questions about the problem. This leads students to ask their teachers, "Why are we doing this?" Students will even apply the correct steps in solving a problem and still look to their teacher for confirmation if their response is correct or not. All too often we see that students are not confident in their mathematical thinking. They are unsure of where to start; how to work through stumbling blocks; or why their answers make sense. This lack of confidence is problematic as students look to the teacher to *help* them decide on the next steps. This lack of confidence also means we have students who are **passive learners**. Students demonstrate little independence. These are red flags we see in many, if not all, grade levels.

There is a disconnect between our **instructional goals** and how we frame the learning experiences our students have in mathematics. It seems students are *doing mathematics* instead of *thinking mathematically*. I believe that teachers go above and beyond to ensure their students have quality experiences with mathematics. So, why are we still seeing students approaching problems by rote instead of through **meaning-making**? Why do students depend on their teachers to help them identify the next steps in a problem, or to explain the rationale of how these concepts will help them outside of school?

For too long, mathematical instruction and learning has been disconnected from students' lived experiences. It seems that what happens in the classroom does not apply to the world we live in. Of course, this is problematic because it may significantly reduce students' engagement level. If students cannot see the purpose of the mathematics, they will have more reasons to disengage from the problem or work through any stumbling blocks. Students need to see the relevance of the problem, make sense of it, and approach it from a meaning-making perspective. We often ask students, "Does your response make sense?" How can they answer this if the problem is irrelevant?

Students are Active Learners

When we provide our students with opportunities to connect mathematics to their everyday lives and to use mathematics to make sense of the world, we give our students an opportunity to understand concepts and apply problem-solving techniques to situations.

I believe that we are close to addressing the issues I referenced earlier. I know this because I have turned things around in my own classroom and have assisted others in doing the same in theirs. The solution is to recognize that we are on a journey, on a continuum. Now it is time to *tweak* how we approach **problem solving** by adjusting the questions we give our students. By changing the questions or tasks we provide students, we put more responsibility on them. They move from *doing mathematics* to *thinking mathematically*. When we provide our students with opportunities to connect mathematics to their everyday lives and to use mathematics to make sense of the world, we give our students an opportunity to understand concepts and apply problem-solving techniques to situations. When this connection is made students will experience culturally relevant mathematics.

Within such an approach, student thinking is *mathematized* as they become confident and capable math learners. By **mathematized**, I mean that student thinking is infused with mathematics, both in how they understand the problem and in how they approach the solution. It goes beyond literal understanding and graduates to how decisions are made, rationalized, communicated, and assessed. Students become independent critical thinkers who are flexible and creative. They can better communicate their understanding of a concept and situation. They recognize that problem solving is a fluid process whereby they are constantly checking for meaning.

The strategies within this book were developed based on evidence, in theory and practice. All mathematical concepts are straightforward. You can apply many of these concepts in your classroom right away. Examples of these strategies, currently being used in many classrooms, are shared in the book. We get first-hand accounts from teachers and students recalling their experiences. Work samples are also presented showing the strategies at work.

This book is intended to meet you where you are on your journey as a teacher who is teaching problem-solving skills. The concepts and examples will help you identify and apply instructional strategies. My goal is to help you identify how to remove what is not working so you can reach your instructional goals. When you apply these concepts, you will not have more work but will instead be able to work differently.

The book begins by distinguishing two categories of problems, defined and ill-defined. We will examine how we have often provided students with only defined problems. Defined problems are the problems that students are assigned with a traditional approach to problem solving. While the work of George Polya, who introduces the four principles to problem solving (discussed later in the book) is suitable, there are still aspects that can be strengthened in terms of instruction and learning. Through examining ill-defined problems, we can acknowledge that traditional problem solving falls short. For ill-defined problems, instruction and learning must provide students with opportunities to mathematically model their thinking and solutions. Throughout this book, I will highlight how mathematizing student thinking requires students to apply meaning when engaging with real-life scenarios within a fluid process. This will prove that they are in fact, capable and confident math learners.

Collective Problem

As I previously stated, we have a collective problem in our classrooms. Even though students are demonstrating success during lessons, solving practice questions, and taking tests, they are finding it difficult to move toward the next step of independence in their learning. I have heard, all too often, that students solve questions when engaging in practice, but cannot apply this learning in another context or later in the year. In fact, when students are given a question that represents a concept from earlier in the year, they will often raise their hand and wait for a teacher to either tell them what the problem is about or ask for a strategy that can be used to reach a solution. This is a passive approach to learning. Students rely on the teacher to make the decisions for them in solving the question. We must ask ourselves if students understand the mathematical questions they are given and if they find it difficult to apply their knowledge.

If we see this in only a few of our students, we can deduce that there is an issue with a student's learning. However, if many of our students are having the same issues across multiple classrooms, from year-to-year, we can deduce that there is an instructional issue. Students are approaching mathematics as formulaic. Students are working through assigned problems without taking the time or being able to question if their response to the problem makes sense. In the end we see students undertaking the task of solving a problem but unable to see the bigger picture that the problem presents.

Consider the following comments from teachers who have seen their students' inability to understand mathematical concepts or recognize if their work has the right answer.

> **Even though students are demonstrating success during lessons, solving practice questions, and taking tests, they are finding it difficult to move toward the next step of independence in their learning.**

PRIMARY EXAMPLE: A TEACHER EXPLAINS

Students will not attempt to work through a task independently. Once they experience discomfort, they will raise their hand and wait for me to come to their desk. When I try to guide them through the questions, they say that they don't know what to do. Students will sit at their desks and wait it out.

I see this year after year, regardless of the different grades I have taught. My students will do well on an individual test, but when given a task that includes the same concept down the road, they are stumped. When they are told what the concept being explored is, they can work through it. However, when they must consider which concept to apply to a given problem, they struggle to the point of giving up.

I don't see critical thinking in my students when it's time to solve a problem. They aren't fully grasping what the problem is about and they have difficulty getting started. Many times, students want me to tell them what the problem is asking. If I tell them, then they can do the computations to arrive at the solution. However, they have difficulty understanding a problem and figuring out what it's about and what steps to take to solve it.

It is important to consider how students view mathematics and themselves as learners. Students explain their issues with solving problems.

Sometimes I find it hard to think of another way to solve a problem. After I read it, I will think of a plan I could use to find the answer. If the plan doesn't work, I can't think of another plan. It's hard to find one plan. I don't know how to find more than one if I need to.

I hear the teacher say it a lot, check to see if your answer makes sense. I don't know how to do that. I don't know what answer would make sense. It's hard because when I'm given a problem, I read it, find the numbers, and try to find the answer. I don't know how to explain how I solved the problem. Sometimes, I think I did great but find out my answers are mostly wrong.

It's frustrating. I have a graphic organizer that I use when problem solving, and it shows me the four steps to take. I can usually fill in each space, but I still don't understand it. Isn't the graphic organizer supposed to help me understand it? If I can do all the steps, why aren't I always right?

Based on the descriptions and comments above, it appears we need to recognize that what is missing in the classroom are skills that go beyond just literal thinking. Simply applying a process without seeing the bigger picture isn't enough. We don't want mathematics to become a series of steps that are just checked off a list. We want students to engage with a problem and to self-monitor their thinking as it relates to solving the problem. Instead, it seems that students are going through isolated steps with little understanding of how the steps are connected to overall problem solving.

Moving forward, we want students to be critical thinkers. They should be able to communicate their understanding, be creative and flexible in approaching a problem, and have **autonomy** in the decisions they make when framing, supporting, and consolidating their understanding. In short, we want our students to become independent learners who *think mathematically,* a skill set needed for the twenty-first century. So, why are students not demonstrating the goals that we set for them? In trying to answer this question, we must first consider our own instructional practices and then move onto examining the problems we provide them under the guise of problem solving.

Instructional Practices May Not Match Instructional Goals

Teachers have an instructional goal to support students to be problem solvers. However, do their instructional practices align with this goal? Far too often, problem solving is taught to be a linear process—following specific steps working through a problem. This approach is too simple. Where does problem solving come in? Let's think about how we approach problem solving in the classroom.

What we know is that our students are struggling with independence and *thinking mathematically* when solving problems. Much of what they are assigned in mathematics resembles blocked practice (Costello, 2021; Rohrer, 2009). **Blocked practice** is where all practice questions focus on the same concept. Typically, this concept is the goal of the lesson. Taking this idea of blocked practice further, let's consider the steps involved. Traditionally, the teacher would provide an opportunity for students to explore a concept. This exploration could be in the form of a mini-lesson facilitated by the teacher, using student work samples as the basis of discussion, or a **think aloud**. Following this, students would be provided multiple questions that would require them to perform the procedure outlined within the concept. In essence, students can solve a problem without completely understanding what it is about. All that is required is for them to identify the pattern in the problems and then pick out numbers to apply to the procedure.

Mathematics consists of a web of ideas that support one another.

When thinking about blocked practice, students encounter math concepts in a "one and done" manner. Concepts are treated in isolation and not many connections are addressed. When treating concepts in isolation, we remove the authenticity of mathematics. Mathematics consists of a web of ideas that support one another. When we remove this interconnectivity, we remove the meaning. And, when we remove meaning, we remove opportunities for critical thinking, creativity, autonomy, and communication. What we are left with is a math instructional approach that relies on **rote learning**. Students check-off steps instead of connecting and communicating their understanding and cannot explain any stumbling blocks.

Students miss out on a big opportunity. They should be able to apply their knowledge within a context where they can take a moment to understand the problem, consider an appropriate strategy from a range of possibilities, and use meaning-making to judge the rationale of their response. How many times in our everyday lives do we experience problems within a blocked practice structure?

We want to remove the barriers students face and make mathematics relevant to their everyday experiences. We want mathematics to be meaningful for students.

Little, if any. We want to remove the barriers students face and make mathematics relevant to their everyday experiences. We want mathematics to be meaningful for students. As such, we want them to be confident and capable math learners who can apply their mathematical understanding to solve a range of problems.

Consider the following comments from teachers highlighting the misalignment between their instructional practices and their instructional goals.

PRIMARY EXAMPLE: A TEACHER EXPLAINS

I approach problem solving using a gradual release of responsibility. I use the "We Do, You Do" approach. This involves a lot of model, model, model. While students seem to be able to understand how to do things after I model them, they aren't showing this when working on their own. They will constantly ask me to answer the first question of a practice set so that they can apply a similar process to the remainder of the problems. What I have figured out is that my approach isn't working. My students have trouble problem solving on their own. They always want me to help them and give them hints.

ELEMENTARY EXAMPLE: A TEACHER EXPLAINS

I give students lots of questions and they do well. In fact, on unit tests all students tend to meet grade level. When I assign a problem that they haven't seen in a while, they struggle, and I don't mean productive struggle. I see a sea of raised hands from students who want to know what the problem is about and how to solve it. Something isn't working and I don't know how to fix it.

INTERMEDIATE EXAMPLE: A TEACHER EXPLAINS

It's tough to address all the curriculum in a grade. I make sure to follow the yearly plan, but I feel that something is missing. I don't have time to revisit curriculum outcomes because when I do, many students don't know what to do and ask a lot of questions. I can't take up time teaching the same concepts over and over. I am confused because they could do it earlier in the year.

Students have provided comments to coincide with their teachers' frustrations below.

PRIMARY EXAMPLE: A STUDENT EXPLAINS

Before we do problems in class, the teacher solves one on the whiteboard. When we work on the problems she assigns us, she leaves her work on the board. I always look at her work to know the steps that I need to do to solve the problems we are assigned.

I like it when we use the math book in class. When we are assigned problems to do for practice, I usually look at the title of the lesson and that tells me what I have to do to solve all of the problems. It usually says what the problems are going to be about, like addition of decimals, multiplication of two-digit by two-digit. The way the problems are arranged is that they get harder as you get into higher numbers. But, each one still is about the same thing.

I got all the questions right on the fractions test we had. The first part was easy because we just had to multiply the two fractions that were given. When I finished all the questions, I saw that each story problem had two fractions in them. I didn't even read the story problems, I just took the two fractions and multiplied them. The teacher said that I am doing really well in math.

While our instructional goal is for students to be independent critical thinkers when they solve problems, we must consider whether our instructional practices align with this goal. Earlier we discussed relying on the gradual release of a blocked practice structure may be a contradiction to our goals. Through such an approach to instruction, we are removing meaning from math and enabling our students to solve problems without understanding the mathematics embedded within the problem.

Are the Assigned Questions Part of the Problem?

The problems we assign our students play a role in supporting them as either passive learners or as independent problem solvers.

The problems we assign our students play a role in supporting them as either passive learners or as independent problem solvers. It is not enough that they merely perform calculations in mathematics. It is imperative that they are provided real-life problems so that they can apply a meaning-making perspective to their problem solving. When engaged in real-life problems, students will be able to apply their experiences to help frame, support, and consolidate their understanding.

Too often, students are provided **close-ended questions**. These types of questions have one correct response—right or wrong. When only one solution exists students may not feel comfortable taking risks when engaging with the problem.

Open-ended questions are better. Open-ended questions provide more flexibility in terms of there being a variety of strategies available to use when solving the problem and the possibility of there being multiple solutions. Although, I want to stress that there is a degree to the openness of a question. If the degree of openness in an open-ended question is limited, students may still not feel comfortable to take risks in working through a strategy to solve the problem—resulting in the same hesitation and disengagement that we see in close-ended questions.

Examples of students' work is provided to highlight assigned close-ended and open-ended questions. Within these samples, please pay close attention to the comments made by the students and teachers.

PRIMARY STUDENT: A WORK SAMPLE

Using twelve base-ten blocks, represent a number that is much bigger than 50 but a little less than 235.

- The student randomly selected twelve blocks. The blocks were as follows:
  - 8 units and 4 rods. This represented 8 + 40 = 48.
- When the teacher asked the student if they solved the problem, the student responded with "I think."
- The student, after looking at the base-ten blocks, said "I don't know." The student gave up because they weren't sure what the problem was asking them to do.

ELEMENTARY STUDENT: A WORK SAMPLE

The school yearbook committee had 25 student members. Of these 25, 15 were first-year members. If each student was responsible for taking thirty pictures for the yearbook, how many pictures would be included in the yearbook?

- The student read the problem three times. After the second read-through, the student highlighted the two references: 25 and 15.
- From this work the student multiplied 25 by 15 to find a product of 375.
- The teacher asked the student why she highlighted the numbers 25 and 15. The student responded that she knew the numbers were important and that she was told to highlight the important information in the problem.
- The teacher then asked the student why she multiplied 25 by 15. The student responded that she also highlighted the word *each* and that this would mean that she should multiply.
- The teacher asked if the student double-checked her work to see if it was correct. The student said that it had to be because there were two numbers and that *each* meant she needed to multiply.

INTERMEDIATE STUDENT: A WORK SAMPLE

A group of thirty-eight artists performed at the local fair. After the fair, twelve artists went to a restaurant for pizza. While at the restaurant, each of the artists ate 1/3 of a pizza. How much pizza was eaten at the restaurant?

- The student looked at the problem and put her pencil down.
- The teacher asked what the first step would be to solve the problem. The student said they weren't sure because they didn't know what the problem was about and didn't know if their work would be right or wrong so why bother trying.
- The teacher asked why they wouldn't be able to assess the reasons supporting their work. The student said they wouldn't know what would make sense if ever they were in a similar situation as in the problem.

From these three work samples students were assigned some open-ended and close-ended problems, yet there was no more than formulaic thinking applied to the work. It is not enough for students to solve the problem by simply applying steps. Steps need to be considered in relation to one another and to the problem. When this does not happen, students cannot approach a solution from a thinking perspective. For the intermediate student, they chose not to work toward a solution because the problem was not relevant to their experiences outside of the classroom. The student understood that traditionally there is only one correct response in the assigned problems. They chose not to take the risk in working through the problem. The three work samples did not have any evidence of *thinking mathematically*.

The work samples presented little opportunity for critical thinking and creativity. The questions—close-ended and open-ended—limited students from making connections to their everyday lives. When the relevance is removed from problem solving so is the autonomy of students' engagement levels.

Removing Barriers Between Mathematics and the Real World

How can we move forward? Sometimes, our instructional practices may not align with our instructional goals, so what can be done? The first step is to define what problem solving looks like. Our goal is for students to problem solve and connect how mathematics plays a role in their lives. Currently how math is presented in the class is disconnected to what students experience out of school. Now, we must reconsider the instructions and problems we assign.

The biggest barrier students face is connecting what happens in the classroom to the real world. They need to make relevant connections with what they learn and what they experience. We are limiting them from developing critical thinking skills and applying this to solving mathematical problems. Problem solving requires some creativity. You can't just take linear steps to get to the answer. Students cannot take ownership of the problem or apply their own experiences to make sense of it and solve the problem. They are not able to communicate their strategy to solve the problem or connect to similar strategies others used in the classroom.

Take a moment to recognize that we have been presenting mathematics in a linear way, void of purpose and relevancy to students. We need to realign our instructional practices so that students can see the beauty of mathematics. Provide students with opportunities to see how mathematics is all around them and that it can be applied to make sense of their world and assist them in solving issues. The faster we come to this realization the faster we will see students engaging in mathematics meaningfully. You will no longer hear "Why are we doing this?" once they start to apply their own experiences to the mathematical problems that are relevant to them.

When we approach mathematics as relevant and purposeful, we expand the definition of problem solving. Then, we will include real-life situations and investigations that are meaningful for students. Students will take autonomy in working through these problems and applying a meaning-making approach to problem solving. Students will be engaged in their learning and care about solving mathematical problems.

We need to realign our instructional practices so that students can see the beauty of mathematics. Provide students with opportunities to see how mathematics is all around them and that it can be applied to make sense of their world and assist them in solving issues.

When we remove the barrier between mathematics and the real-world, we move away from students following a formulaic process to come to a solution toward having students *think* mathematically. Students can think about the problem carefully by considering it from multiple perspectives; applying various strategies in solving the problem; assessing their thinking to ensure they are approaching a meaningful solution; and gaining confidence to share their learning. Within this shift from *doing* mathematics to *thinking* mathematically, students are engaged in an iterative process of problem solving. They constantly go back and forth, from the problem to their understanding of it and how they are solving it. It is not a linear method of completing step one, then moving to step two and so on. Students are constantly checking for meaning and assessing their work and thinking about the whole problem. It allows students to see the big picture as they work toward solving the problem.

When we provide students opportunities to engage in mathematics that reflects their lives, we tap into their sense of wonder. And, in doing so, we encourage students to question and investigate both the problem and their understanding of mathematics. The more this is done the more students flex their critical thinking and creativity skills. Independent thinking is a required skill in the twenty-first century.

Consider the following comments from teachers that highlight the need for removing the barrier between mathematics and the real-world. These examples will expand our definition of problem solving thereby influencing our approach to instruction.

> **When we provide students opportunities to engage in mathematics that reflects their lives, we tap into their sense of wonder. And, in doing so, we encourage students to question and investigate both the problem and their understanding of mathematics.**

PRIMARY EXAMPLE: A TEACHER EXPLAINS

It's about connecting math and the real world. I want my students to see how math is all around them. By doing this, they are making connections and making meaning. They can use this to support their understanding so that when working through a problem they can assess their work themselves instead of always relying on me to tell them if they are right or not.

ELEMENTARY EXAMPLE: A TEACHER EXPLAINS

We are focusing on making math meaningful. We're engaging with investigations that support students in developing their critical thinking and flexibility. My students are becoming much more independent and can work through stumbling blocks. As soon as they are given a task that resembles their experiences outside of the classroom they are motivated to work toward a solution.

INTERMEDIATE EXAMPLE: A TEACHER EXPLAINS

What is the purpose of math? Why are we doing this? I kept hearing these questions from my students. Since I started to emphasize how mathematics can be used to make sense of the world around us and how it can be used to solve real-world issues, students are seeing its relevance and are motivated to work through the task.

Let's see how students are experiencing the approach to solve problems.

PRIMARY EXAMPLE: A STUDENT EXPLAINS

We just worked on a problem where we had to think of what equipment we should have for our new playground. We did surveys, tallies, graphs, additions, and problem solving. We did lots to solve the one problem. It took us two days and we loved it. It was about stuff that mattered.

ELEMENTARY EXAMPLE: A STUDENT EXPLAINS

I used to ask the teacher why she gave us the story problems she did. No one cared about the story or what the answer was. It was just something to do. Since we started doing investigations that involved things we care about in the world, I like doing math. It makes sense and I can figure out a plan to solve the problem. I think about things in my life and sometimes things from other subjects. These help me make sense of the problem and work through it. I also like how there isn't just one right answer, and everybody can show they know math.

INTERMEDIATE EXAMPLE: A STUDENT EXPLAINS

We worked on a problem for the past two days. It was something that we weren't used to. We had to figure out the route for a tourist who wanted to visit different places in a province. We had to decide on the route, figure out the time needed to make the trip, explain why we chose that route, and calculate the cost of the trip. While we struggled to understand it at first, it was great to see how we figured out the route and to see the routes that other groups selected. We did a lot of math.

Relevancy not only promotes engagement and autonomy, but it promotes student understanding of concepts and seeing how they can be applied to solve problems within their world.

What a difference it makes when students are engaged in mathematics and when they find the task to be relevant. By removing the barriers between mathematics in the classroom and the real-world, we allow students to approach their problem solving from a meaning-making perspective that is supported by their experiences. Removing barriers eliminates any need for students to question why they must solve the problems they are assigned and when they are ever going to use this concept outside of school. Relevancy not only promotes engagement and autonomy, but it promotes student understanding of concepts and seeing how they can be applied to solve problems within their world. Students begin to *think mathematically* and problem solve within an iterative process instead of approaching the problem superficially.

Adjusting Instruction to Include Defined and Ill-Defined Problems

By removing the barrier between mathematics in the classroom and the real world, we need to adjust the problems we are providing students. It is evident that the traditional approach to word/story problems is falling short. Simply adding words to a math question and providing a context is not enough. We must take the next step and assign problems that are meaningful and relevant to the lives of our students. We need to have rich tasks in the classroom.

Rich tasks are questions that have common characteristics. There must be:

- Problems that are accessible to all learners. Having multiple points of entry enables students to engage with the problem and make sense of it.
- Problems that are reflective of real life for the students.
- Opportunities for multiple approaches and representation. This promotes individuality and creativity.
- Collaboration and discussion present. Communication is a significant **mathematical process**. Students should collaborate and discuss their thinking.
- A level of engagement present so that students are curious about the problem.
- Opportunities for extension in place to allow students to continue exploration if they choose.

Rich tasks provide students the opening to *think mathematically* instead of simply *doing mathematics*. It is important that we be mindful of the problems we assign students and take the time to consider whether the problems are representative of rich tasks. Now, there is a range that exists when we think about rich tasks. At opposite ends of this range are defined problems and ill-defined problems.

Defined problems are those problems that we typically observe and experience in the classroom.

When looking at defined problems, the opportunity for flexibility and creativity may be limited. Students are provided a problem where the goal is explicitly communicated. Students have all the necessary information to solve the problem and there is either a unique or a limited range of possible solutions. It is the job of students to use the given information, to identify an effective strategy (typically only a few strategies can be applied to find the solution), and to arrive at the predetermined solution. By limiting the flexibility and creativity of students, their level of engagement will be diminished. Within such a scenario is where questions such as "Why are we doing this question?" or "When are we going to use this?" may come up. Simply adding context to everyday examples does not make them relevant or meaningful. It is more than that.

Consider how defined problems relate to the real world. How many times in our own lives have we encountered a problem outside of school that presents us with all the necessary information and has a unique solution? Most times, when we encounter problems outside of school, the information we are given is limited and there may be multiple solutions to solve that problem. This is when our critical thinking skills are exercised. When faced with such obstacles we rely on critical thinking, flexibility, creativity, and autonomy to problem solve.

Now, let's consider the other side of the range when thinking about rich tasks. Ill-defined problems are less common in the classroom, but can be a gamechanger in terms of teachers reaching their instructional goal of making mathematics relevant and having students *think mathematically*. Ill-defined problems are missing one or more of the parameters that characterize defined problems. For example, an ill-defined problem reflects the problems we encounter in everyday-life. Rarely, do we encounter a problem where we are provided with all the necessary information at the start. Instead, we have to dig into the situation and

Simply adding context to everyday examples does not make them relevant or meaningful. It is more than that. Consider how defined problems relate to the real world.

consider many factors. It is rare that we have a clearly stated goal. The goal is determined by the person who is solving the problem. This is where engagement comes into play and when individuals must use their autonomy in working through a problem. Ill-defined problems do not have a unique solution but rather many possible options. What is important is that the response makes sense and that it addresses the question students encounter.

In short, ill-defined problems are messy. Problems are not simply black or white, there is more to understanding the problem, working through the problem, and arriving at a response. Ill-defined problems resemble those that we come across in the real world. Ill-defined problems are relevant to students and highlight how mathematics is embedded in the world to solve real-world issues. With ill-defined problems students must take an active stance in their learning. They cannot rely on the teacher for answers or expecting the facts to be presented to them like in traditional math problems. They need to be independent. They need to be thinking about the problems they encounter from the perspective of their experiences and the world they live in. Ill-defined problems move students from *doing mathematics* to *thinking mathematically*. Ill-defined problems require students to mathematize their thinking throughout the entire problem-solving process. This is problem solving moving forward.

In This Book

This introduction has illustrated the complexity associated with problem solving. While our instructional goals are to support students in becoming critical thinkers who are independent and flexible problem solvers, we do not see this happening in our classrooms. Instead, we have many students who are dependent on the teacher to clarify the problem for them, to help them identify next steps, and to determine if their response solves the assigned problem. We are seeing many students, across various grade levels, that are passive and going through the motions by *doing mathematics* instead of *thinking mathematically*. This is not enough. We are doing our students an injustice.

To have students who demonstrate critical thinking, creativity, flexibility, and autonomy in mathematics, we need to adjust our approach to instruction. A new approach requires us to remove any barrier that exists between mathematics in the classroom and the real world. By removing this barrier, we provide students with opportunities to strengthen their ability to approach mathematics from a meaning-making stance instead of approaching mathematics as a sequence of unrelated steps. We make this move by adjusting the problems assigned in the classroom. We move from an instructional approach using defined problems to one that provides students opportunities to engage with defined and ill-defined problems.

By offering students ill-defined problems, we are aware that the traditional four-step process (discussed in Chapter 2) of problem solving is not enough. We need to move problem solving in mathematics toward real-world problem solving. We need to expand problem solving to include mathematical modelling where students engage with problems and mathematize their thinking. Students appreciate and come to see how math surrounds them and how math can be applied to solve issues out in the world. Through mathematical modelling, students take ownership of their learning and strengthen skills, which is a necessity in the twenty-first century.

Ill-defined problems are relevant to students and highlight how mathematics is embedded in the world to solve real-world issues. With ill-defined problems students must take an active stance in their learning.

This book will walk you through the process of expanding problem solving to include mathematical modelling. You will be supported through this journey of making mathematics meaningful for students. As the teacher, you will move from hearing questions such as "Why are we doing this?" or "When are we ever going to use this?" to facilitating learning experiences where students are engaged, take autonomy, and make meaning with mathematics. In short, it will be the students who are *thinking mathematically* instead of you constantly giving them hints to move from one step to the next. Let's begin mathematizing student thinking.

Within this book, I introduce an approach to mathematics instruction and learning that goes beyond superficial learning. In sharing this approach, I will provide problems from the perspective of both teachers and students outlining their struggles, and work samples to aid in solving these issues. The basis of the chapters will be to ground our conversation and journey in the classroom so that you can see the work in action.

Mathematical modelling begins in kindergarten and develops throughout primary, elementary, and intermediate grade levels.

Throughout the text I will include examples from three grade level bands: Primary (Kindergarten to Grade 3); Elementary (Grade 4 to Grade 6); and Intermediate (Grade 7 to Grade 8). Mathematical modelling begins in kindergarten and develops throughout primary, elementary, and intermediate grade levels. Mathematical modelling is not meant for later studies, it is meant for students at these levels. If we want to see changes in your students understanding, we need to take the first step. Students can mathematize their thinking from their first day of education. Let's start today.

CHAPTER 1

Redefining Problems

When we think about mathematics we tend to think of problems. As stated in the Introduction, our goal is to make students problem solvers. Let's not glaze over the term **problem**. We should not take for granted what a problem means to teachers and students, or how their perspectives differ. Teachers have varied definitions of what a problem entails and have provided some explanations.

THOUGHTS FROM PRIMARY TEACHERS

- "A problem is something that will make students think outside the box. It is something that they haven't seen before."
- "A problem can be anything and everything. What's important is that students don't know the answer right away."

THOUGHTS FROM ELEMENTARY TEACHERS

- "Problems are about students working through stumbling blocks to reach a solution. It's about them persevering and determining how to arrive at a solution that's not initially evident."
- "Problems are about trial and error. They are about people figuring out what is needed and then finding a plan that will get them to the solution."

- "A problem is something that requires students to think critically. They need to take time to understand the problem, craft a plan, carry out the plan, and reflect on their work."
- "Problems come in all shapes and sizes. Too often, problems seem to be focused on a number, but this is too limiting. We need to consider problems in all areas of math."

It is apparent that teachers connect problems with critical thinking, perseverance, and thinking outside the box. Now, let's see how students responded to the same question.

- "Problems make us think. They are hard."
- "Problems can be just numbers."

- "We usually get problems at the end of the math block. We use what we learn to figure it out."
- "Word problems are the problems we get. If you look for key words like altogether, share, and groups of, you will know what you need to do to solve the problem."

- "Problems are frustrating. Most times problems are about useless things that we don't care about."
- "I used to think problems in math had to have words, but they don't. Sometimes when I get a question with just numbers and have to find the value of the variable, that's a problem."

Clearly teachers and students have different perspectives about what defines a problem. Teachers view problems from the perspective of thinking and perseverance, while students take the view that problems means word problems. The two perspectives are not synonymous. Simply assigning a task with the word "problem" in its title does not ensure that students will problem solve.

What Is a Problem?

Consider whether the following questions. Are they problems or not?

David has 23 hockey cards. He loses some while cleaning his room. He now has 16 cards. How many cards did David lose?

~~~~~~

$? = 8 - 2$

~~~~~~

What is the value of the underlined digit? 5<u>3</u>8

~~~~~~

What is the missing element?

$+ + \# + + \# + \bigcirc \# + +$

Find the area.

46 m

4 m

~~~~~~

Compare the following numbers using < , > or =

$\frac{3}{4} \bigcirc \frac{7}{8}$

~~~~~~

Find the missing value

x	y
4	9
6	13
3	7
9	?

~~~~~~

Measure the angle.

Solve
$38 = 6x - 4$

~~~~~~

Which of the following nets, if any, would produce a cube?

~~~~~~

Compare and contrast mean and mode.

~~~~~~

Alli places two blue and two yellow marbles in a bag. Find the probability of drawing two blue marbles if the first one is not returned before drawing the second.

Which of the examples did you consider a problem? Why? When you were considering whether the questions were problems or not, did the assigned grade level make a difference?

It is important to recognize that what some people may consider a problem may not be seen as one by someone else. Does previous experience play a role? Is this a novel situation for students, or have they seen it multiple times before?

> We must be aware when thinking about what constitutes a problem. There is a distinction to be made between practice and problems.

We must be aware when thinking about what constitutes a problem. There is a distinction to be made between practice and problems. In terms of practice, students approach the question decisively and can easily distinguish what is being asked and find a solution. There is more unknown associated with a problem. A problem is present when the student has a goal but does not know how to achieve that goal.

Let's consider what a problem *actually* is. When examining problems, there are three common characteristics: initial state; goal state; and obstacles (Greenwald, 2000).

Initial State

Initial state is the state that students are presented with at the onset of the problem. For example, in a word problem this would be the scenario that is presented to the student. In an equation, this would be the *what* the student would have to solve to determine the value of the unknown. In a table, it is the information that the student is presented with. In a pattern, it is the sequence (whether repeating, increasing, or decreasing) that students are presented. The initial state is what the student is presented with as the starting point of the problem-solving process.

Goal State

The **goal state** is what is achieved and desired by the student. It is the preferred outcome. For example, in a word problem it is the question that students must be able to answer. In a table of values, it is the pattern that the student must recognize in the values and/or use to identify the unknown value. In a pattern, it may be to recognize the pattern (whether it is repeating, increasing, or decreasing), identify what comes next, and/or correct any inaccuracy in the pattern.

Obstacles

Obstacles, also referred to as stumbling blocks, are what happens between the initial state and the goal state. An obstacle would engage students in **productive struggle**. Initially, students would not be sure how to move from the initial state to the goal state. This may include the student having difficulty understanding the problem, identifying a plan of action to overcome the obstacle, and/or enacting this plan of action. Problem solving is the thinking that happens to work through the obstacles.

Let's take a closer look at the problems we saw earlier putting the three characteristics into practice and examining how they fit into the problems. It is important to note that a student's previous learning is taken into consideration for these problems so they may not be novel. It could be an opportunity to practice instead of problem solving.

PUTTING IT INTO PRACTICE: PRIMARY EXAMPLES

David has 23 hockey cards. He loses some while cleaning his room. He now has 16 cards. How many cards did David lose?

Initial State: David has 23 hockey cards. He loses some while cleaning his room. He now has 16 cards.
Goal State: How many cards did David lose?
Obstacle: Determine the strategy (or strategies) needed and apply it to find out how many cards David lost.

~~~~~~

$? = 8 - 2$

Initial State: $= 8 - 2$
Goal State: ?
Obstacle: Determine the strategy needed and apply it to find out the value represented by the ? .

~~~~~~

What is the missing element?

+ + # + + # + ○ # + +

Initial State: + + # + + # + ○ # + +
Goal State: What is the missing element?
Obstacle: Determine the pattern and identify the missing symbol.

PUTTING IT INTO PRACTICE: ELEMENTARY EXAMPLES

Find the area.

46 m

	4 m

Initial State: 46 m

	4 m

Goal State: Find the area.
Obstacle: Determine the strategy needed and apply it to find the area.

~~~~~~

Compare the following numbers using < , > or =

$\frac{3}{4}$ ○ $\frac{7}{8}$

Initial State: $\frac{3}{4}$ ○ $\frac{7}{8}$
Goal State: Compare the following numbers using < , > or =
Obstacle: Determine the strategy needed to compare the two fractions; then decide which symbol to record in the circle.

~~~~~~

Find the missing value.

x	y
4	9
6	13
3	7
9	?

Initial State:

x	y
4	9
6	13
3	7
9	?

Goal State: Find the missing value.
Obstacle: Determine the pattern rule (expression) for x to y and then apply this to find the number represented by the ? .

Solve.
$38 = 6x - 4$

Initial State: $38 = 6x - 4$
Goal State: Solve.
Obstacle: Determine the strategy needed and apply it to find out the value represented by x.

~~~~~~

Which of the following nets, if any, would produce a cube?

Initial State:

Goal State: Which of the following nets, if any, would produce a cube?
Obstacle: Determine if the given nets make a cube; then share which one(s) do.

~~~~~~

Alli places two blue and two yellow marbles in a bag. Find the probability of drawing two blue marbles if the first one is not returned before drawing the second.

Initial State: Alli places two blue and two yellow marbles in a bag… if the first one is not returned before drawing the second.
Goal State: Find the probability of drawing two blue marbles.
Obstacle: Determine the strategy (or strategies) needed to figure out the probability.

Strengthening the Problem

In the problems we have seen, we notice that there was little connection to the lives of students and few opportunities for engagement and interest. This was intentional to highlight how we can strengthen the problems that we are presenting to students. Consider the following characteristics of **rich tasks**: accessibility; real-life experience; interesting and engaging opportunities for creativity and individuality; variety of approaches and representations; opportunities for collaboration and discussion; and extending learning (Butler Wolf, 2015; National Council of Teachers of Mathematics, 2014; Van de Walle, Karp, Bay-Williams, & McGarvey, 2017).

Accessibility

Accessibility for learners is a significant aspect of rich tasks. Students can come with a wide range of learning abilities and needs. Tasks must be created with multiple possible points of entry and exit so that all types of students can approach the problem from various perspectives, such as mathematical understanding, experience, and foundational knowledge. By having possible **points of entry**, all students can engage in the task and work toward a solution. For possible **points of exit**, tasks that provide students with opportunities to arrive at various responses that could be considered correct. It increases the probability of successfully completing the task.

Real-life Experiences

When the problem can be compared to real-life experiences, students view the task as more meaningful and worthwhile. When students can recognize the situation and problem, they are more likely to have greater engagement and motivation. This decreases the number of stumbling blocks and lessens the chances of giving up.

Interesting and Engaging

By being able to relate to the problem, student interest and engagement with the problem are stronger. When students are motivated to solve the problem, they feel a need to continue their exploration and discovery. Curiosity about the situation and solution increases and students are eager reach the solution.

Creativity and Individuality

Through an increase in exploration and discovery, the opportunity for individuality is strengthened. Students are encouraged to be creative in their approach to solving the problem. This creativity could be in how they approach the problem, the strategy or strategies they choose as their plan of action, and the action they take. Individuality and creativity used to apply toward mathematical reasoning is as important as the solution itself. The thinking that students apply in the process cannot be understated. It exemplifies their understanding of the problem and the mathematics that they are applying to reach a solution.

> When the problem can be compared to real-life experiences, students view the task as more meaningful and worthwhile.

A Variety of Approaches and Representations

Problems that lend themselves to a variety of approaches and representations provide an opportunity for students to approach mathematics from a different perspective. By having this openness, there is an increase in the likelihood of more students having success. Through a variety of approaches and representations, students will be confident that there is more than one correct way to approach the problem. This, in turn, encourages students to persevere in determining a plan of action to apply to problem solving.

Collaboration and Discussion

With so many approaches and representations available the opportunity for collaboration and discussion increases among students. By collaborating and discussing mathematics with others, they are strengthening both their understanding of the problem and of other ways to approach a solution. Collaboration and discussion supports metacognition when students must clarify their thinking about the problem and their approach to solving it. They can also reflect on how their thinking is similar to their classmates. Therefore, student thinking is strengthened as is the communicative ability of students.

Extending Learning

The rich task is a problem that provides students with the chance to connect meaning to a familiar lived experience. Relevant problems enable students to engage and work through stumbling blocks and apply creative and individual approaches to solve problems.

A final characteristic of rich tasks that cannot be understated is the opportunity for extended learning. When problems have the openness to allow students the opportunity to extend their learning, mathematical understanding is strengthened. One such example of this extension of learning is being able to make connections amongst mathematical concepts. Through making connections amongst concepts, students build a deeper mathematical understanding as they apply a network of concepts to make sense of the problem and make sense of how to solve the problem. In addition to making connections amongst concepts, students can extend their learning by approaching the problem from a more complex perspective and/or strategy. Through applying a more complex perspective and/or strategy, students can enter the problem from a differing point of entry and can exit the problem from a more complex point of exit. Thereby, students are provided an opportunity to challenge themselves as learners.

The rich task is a problem that provides students with the chance to connect meaning to a familiar lived experience. Relevant problems enable students to engage and work through stumbling blocks and apply creative and individual approaches to solve problems. Rich tasks have multiple points of entry and exit, so there are more ways to apply problem-solving skills. Students can feel more confident talking through their mathematical understanding with their classmates. Now students can move from doing mathematics to thinking mathematically.

Finding Problems

Now that we have considered a problem from the perspective of teachers and students, and have examined what constitutes a problem and a rich task, let's consider where teachers tend to *get* the problems they assign students in the classroom.

- "I find it hard to know just what problem to give my students. I usually look in my guides and on the internet to find problems that I can give my class that they will be able to work on and not have to ask me too many questions."
- "When looking, I think if the problem would be meaningful for students and if they could connect to it. Sometimes, I will use the names of my students in the problem to help them make connections."
- "I usually start with one-step problems and then will move to two-step problems. Sometimes, I find that giving problems more complex than this causes my students to be overwhelmed and just give up."

- "I was told a long time ago that there is no need to recreate the wheel. So, when I need problems, I will look in curriculum, support documents, and program materials. Sometimes it is easy to find the problems to assign, while other times I have to make small revisions to make them accessible for my students. If I can't find problems using those resources, I will search for word problems on the internet."
- "When looking for problems, I will look for word problems that aren't too wordy. I don't want students to have difficulty reading the problems. I am focusing on math not reading."
- "I want word problems that have a structure (start, change, and result unknown). It's important that students experience the different structures of problems."

- "The student textbook is great for problems. I assign the problems in the text because these are the problems they will find on tests and exams. I want them prepared and set up for success."
- "I want problems that have multi-steps (two–to–three) so that students have to think about the process they need to apply to solve the problems. They can't just do the first step and then be finished. They need to know how to use what they figured out to help them in the next part of the problem."
- "It is crucial that students see problems that have information displayed in different ways. For example, students should be able to read information within the word problem, take it from a table, take it from a graph, and take it from a picture. By having these different formats, students will see how information can be presented differently and can strengthen their ability to locate important information."

Regardless of the grade level range above, teachers generally look for problems in the resources they are provided, such as in the curriculum, program materials, and/or course text. When asked for the type of problem teachers select, they were focused on problems that were meaningful, had various structures, and were multi-step. These teachers did have a similar approach. They generally selected from similar sources and chose problems that have varying structures. When considering the variances in problems, all that was referenced was structure and number of steps.

What I want to do next is to situate these responses in the types of problems I have assigned, observed, and/or was told about by educators in primary, elementary, and intermediate grade levels. Using this technique, we will understand more about the types of problems students are assigned and the type of problem-solving experiences students may have in the classroom.

Problems Used in the Classroom

There are many problem types available to assign or share in the classroom. It is important that students experience a variety of problems during their education.

There are many problem types available to assign or share in the classroom. It is important that students experience a variety of problems during their education. I have created a visual that represents the typical problems assigned in the classrooms that I have both observed and worked in over the years.

Procedural	Words-As-Labels	Open-ended	Rich Tasks

I will treat these problem types in isolation so that you have a clear understanding of each type and what they may look like at primary, elementary, and intermediate levels.

Procedural Problems

Once students understand the concepts, they need the opportunity to apply those concepts. This approach to problems is referred to as procedural. **Procedural problems** are ones where the strategy is already identified for students, and they must apply the steps accurately in order to find the solution.

Procedural problems will seem familiar since these were the type of problems we encountered as students during Kindergarten to Grade 8.

PROCEDURAL PROBLEMS: PRIMARY EXAMPLES
Solve: $68 + 15$ Solve: $8 = ? - 3$

PROCEDURAL PROBLEMS: ELEMENTARY EXAMPLES
Solve: $9 + 6 \times 3 - 4$ Solve: $178.23 \div 6$

Solve:
$\frac{2}{3} + \frac{3}{7}$

Solve:
$-3 - (-3)$

As you can see in the procedural problem examples above, there is still a problematic aspect to the questions. While students are aware of what concept is being applied, they must be able to remember and apply the process accurately.

Consider the primary examples—students must recognize that 68 + 15 is an expression that must be solved. And, in the second primary example, students must recognize that they have to preserve equality and determine that the ? in the equation has to represent 11 for both sides of = to be balanced.

The elementary examples, students recognize that an order of operations must be followed to determine the solution. In the second example, the student must divide 178.23 by 6, but they have a choice on how they approach this division problem.

The intermediate problems, students must solve an addition problem involving fractions and then a subtraction problem involving integers.

While each of the primary, elementary, and intermediate examples shown may not seem to be problematic, they are. Although the concept has been identified for students—conversation of equality, the type of operation, order of operations—students must be able to apply these to the problem to arrive at a solution. There is a place for procedural problems, they just cannot be the only type of problem that students are provided.

The three characteristics of problems are present within these examples: initial state, goal state, and obstacles. To clarify, students are pointed to which strategy to apply to overcome the obstacle. In terms of procedural problems, the obstacle is accurately applying the strategy to reach the goal state.

Words-As-Labels Problems

There are similarities and differences between procedural problems and **words-as-labels**. Both problem types have one solution. Whichever problem is used, there is only one solution that the students are working toward. In this case, students are either right or wrong in their final response.

The main distinction between procedural problems and words-as-labels problems is that there are now words in the problem. Words-as-labels problems provide a context for students. Instead of students being explicitly told which strategy to apply—as they are in procedural problems—students must read through the problem and decide which strategy applies to the situation. Words-as-labels problems are commonly referred to as story problems or word problems.

In these problems, words are simply adding labels to the items to be manipulated. Within procedural and words-as-labels problems, there are limited choices for students in applying strategy. While procedural problems indicate the strategy to be applied, students have some variance in how to approach it. For example, in addition contexts, students can apply facts, count from one or count on

There is a place for procedural problems, they just cannot be the only type of problem that students are provided.

to reach the solution. Within words-as-labels problems, students have the same choice once they determine which strategy to apply.

Elijah had a collection of eight marbles. After looking through some of his brother's old toys, Elijah found seven marbles. How many marbles does Elijah now have in his collection?

~~~~~~

Winnie had three fish in the fish tank. Winnie's family bought her more fish for her birthday. Now, there are nine fish in Winnie's fish tank. How many fish did Winnie's family buy her?

~~~~~~

Juan had some stickers to give his friends. He gave four stickers to his friends and he has eight left. How many stickers did Juan have before he gave any to his friends?

~~~~~~

Elizabeth decided to purchase some items from the store. She purchased a book, poster, and crayons. How much did Elizabeth spend?
> Book –$12
> Crayons –$8
> Poster –$9

~~~~~~

Consider the above problem with extraneous information:
Elizabeth decided to purchase some items from the store. She purchased a book, poster, and crayons. How much did Elizabeth spend?
> Book –$12
> Markers –$6
> Crayons –$8
> Poster –$9

~~~~~~

Consider the above problem with an additional step:
Elizabeth had $45 to spend at the store. If Elizabeth purchased a book, poster, and crayons, how much money does she have left?
> Book –$12
> Markers –$6
> Crayons –$8
> Poster –$9

Dane purchased eighteen yearbooks for a cost of $96. If each yearbook was the same price, how much did each cost?

~~~~~~

Talia had seven boxes of books. If each box had 25 books, how many books did Talia have?

~~~~~~

Josef's class had twenty-eight students. Each student raised $50. How much money did Josef's class raise for the fundraiser?

~~~~~~

Consider the above problem with extraneous information:

Josef's class set a goal to raise enough money to purchase 20 soccer balls for the school. Josef's class had twenty-eight students. Each student raised $50. How much money did Josef's class raise for the fundraiser?

~~~~~~

Consider the above problem with an additional step:

Josef's class set a goal to raise enough money to purchase 20 soccer balls for the school. Josef's class had twenty-eight students. Each student raised $50. How much money did Josef's class raise for the fundraiser? If the price of each soccer ball is $40, how much money does Josef's class have left?

Two friends decided to share a pizza. Ethan ate $\frac{2}{5}$ of the pizza and Elias ate $\frac{2}{4}$ of the pizza. How much of the pizza wasn't eaten?

~~~~~~

At the start of the game, the temperature outside the school was 8°C. At the end of the game, the temperature was −4°C. How much did the temperature decrease during the game?

~~~~~~

Alyah's community decided to have a fundraiser and set a goal of $2500. If the community raised $\frac{3}{4}$ of this goal, how much money have they raised so far?

~~~~~~

> *Consider the above problem with extraneous information:*
>
> Alyah's community decided to have a fundraiser and set a goal of $2500. If the community raised $\frac{3}{4}$ of the fundraising goal in a three-month period, how much money have they raised so far?
>
> ~~~~~~
>
> *Consider the above problem with an additional step:*
>
> Alyah's community decided to have a fundraiser and set a goal of $2500. If the community raised $\frac{3}{4}$ of the fundraising goal in a three-month period, how much money have they raised so far? How much money does the community still need to raise to meet its goal?

Words-as-labels provide context, but the problem itself can be adjusted to allow for alternate ways of including information in it.

As observed in the previous primary, elementary, and intermediate words-as-labels examples, there are various ways that the problems can be presented. Words-as-labels provide context, but the problem itself can be adjusted to allow for alternate ways of including information. In the primary example, the price of items is listed. This information could be presented in a list or it could have been written out within the sentence of the problem just like the elementary examples. Another way to introduce these options could be to place them in a diagram of each item with the corresponding price attached.

Another way to write words-as-labels problems is to include extraneous information. This would then allow the students to read through the problem and identify what the problem is about, then distinguish between the relevant and irrelevant information. Extraneous information adds another layer of complexity to the situation.

In addition to adding extraneous information, the problem can be adjusted by including an additional step students must address. By incorporating added steps to a problem, students are required to address multiple steps to reach the solution.

All the words-as-labels problem examples include the three characteristics of a problem: initial state, goal state, and obstacles. Within words-as-labels problems, students must decide which strategy to apply and then take this strategy to overcome the obstacle. This, as compared to procedural problems, is an additional layer of difficulty.

Open-Ended Problems

Open-ended problems, also referred to as open questions, approach instruction and learning from a much wider lens than our previous two problem types. Within open-ended problems, students are provided opportunities for a greater degree of choice in the strategy to use and applying it. For example, as can be seen in the examples of open-ended problems, students are presented with a scenario that allows for flexibility in approaching the problem and how they can determine which strategy to apply and how. Simply put, open-ended problems are tasks put together in such a way that opens up possible answers and many ways to get to the answers (Small, 2013).

The openness of open-ended problems is meant to provide students with multiple points of entry and multiple points of exit. It is about students having choice in how they approach the problem and how they work through it. Such openness is meant to be a source of differentiation so that students at various developmental levels can approach the problem within their zone of proximal development (Small, 2012).

As indicated in the examples provided next, open-ended problems can be presented to multiple student levels and each student can apply their mathematical understanding to the problem so that they can persevere and reach one of the many solutions to the problem.

OPEN-ENDED PROBLEMS: PRIMARY EXAMPLES

What number can you represent using eight base-ten blocks?

~~~~~~

I have two numbers that have a sum of approximately 80. What could the two numbers be?

~~~~~~

Sara is five-years older than her brother. How old could Sara and her brother be?

~~~~~~

A pattern has more green cubes than red cubes. What could the pattern look like?

OPEN-ENDED PROBLEMS: ELEMENTARY EXAMPLES

Which of the following fractions do not belong: $\frac{4}{9}$ $\frac{2}{7}$ $\frac{1}{9}$ $\frac{4}{4}$

~~~~~~

Consider four numbers that are greater than 10 000 but less than 100 000. The sum of the digits in each number is 21. Arrange the four numbers in ascending order.

~~~~~~

The sum of three numbers totalled more than 1000. One of these numbers was more than half of the sum. What could the other two numbers be?

~~~~~~

The perimeter of a rectangle is between 40 cm and 60 cm. The area of this same rectangle is between 100 cm² and 120 cm². What could the length and width of the rectangle be?

The product of two fractions is between half and three-quarters. What could the two fractions be?

~~~~~~

When solving an equation, I determine that the value of **x** is 4. What could the equation be?

~~~~~~

Complete the following statement so that it is true:
20% of _____ is _____

~~~~~~

The sum of two decimal numbers is between 10 and 20 while the product of the same two decimal numbers is between 60 and 70. What could the two decimal numbers be?

The various examples of open-ended problems are meant to highlight how students with various levels of mathematical understanding can approach the problem and work through it to achieve a successful response. The openness allows for students to apply a variety of strategies to the problem. The flexibility that is offered with an open-ended problem is the opportunity for students to add meaning and arrive at a response that addresses the question being asked.

As students work through an open-ended problem, they can apply creativity and flexibility to their thinking. They know that there is not only one prescribed way to approach the problem and it is because of this openness that there is more than one available solution. Flexibility promotes creativity, enabling students to feel less restricted in the strategy they choose to solve the problem. In addition, students have a greater likelihood to persevere. When encountering a stumbling block, students are more likely to work through it because they recognize that there are multiple avenues that they can take to get to a solution. Flexibility means that options are available which encourages students to work through the problem.

A positive aspect of assigning open-ended problems is what it can do for classroom discourse. With multiple points of entry and exit, there is an opportunity for students to share their individual approaches and solutions with one another. By sharing, students will realize that their approach is one of many that can be applied. There is more than one possible solution to the problem they are trying to solve. Sharing strategies and solutions not only supports student reflection and clarity in discovering their own mathematical understanding, but also in how to revise how they think when listening to others' approaches.

Like the other problem types we have discussed, open-ended problems are also comprised of the three characteristics of a problem: initial state, goal state, and obstacles. Students are presented with an initial state and are asked to arrive at the goal state. The emphasis in open-ended problems is that students have more choices in how to overcome obstacles and arrive at the goal state. The goal

Sharing strategies and solutions not only supports student reflection and clarity in discovering their own mathematical understanding, but also in how to revise how they think when listening to others' approaches.

state is quite open since multiple goal states exist. It is not a singular goal state, but instead a goal state that consists of many possibilities.

Rich Tasks

Rich tasks are types of problems that provide students with an opportunity to make meaning within a context that is familiar to their lived experiences. When considering a familiar context, students can recall experiences or situations they have had in and out of school.

Rich tasks are types of problems that provide students with an opportunity to make meaning within a context that is familiar to their lived experiences. When considering a familiar context, students can recall experiences or situations they have had in and out of school. Rich tasks are meant to be opportunities for engagement and interest. Students are afforded the opportunity to select from a variety of approaches and representations as they work toward the solution, where one or more can exist (Butler Wolf, 2015; National Council of Teachers of Mathematics, 2014; Van de Walle, Karp, Bay-Williams, & McGarvey, 2017).

RICH TASK PROBLEMS: PRIMARY EXAMPLES

A Grade 3 classroom of eighteen students had three bookcases. There were three shelves on each bookcase. Each shelf had more books than the number of students in the classroom. How many books were there on the three bookcases?

~~~~~~

Two students were using cube-a-links to make a pattern. One student was making a repeating pattern while the other student was making an increasing pattern. When working on their individual patterns, the students realized that they used the same-coloured cube-a-link for the tenth item in their patterns. Is there a way that they will use the same colour again for the twelfth item in their patterns?

RICH TASK PROBLEMS: ELEMENTARY EXAMPLES

The school soccer team decided to purchase team hoodies. These hoodies were $22 each or 4 for $80. If there were 22 players on the team, how much money would the hoodies cost?

~~~~~~

The local rink had two major programs using the ice surface: figure skating and hockey. Both figure skating and hockey programs agreed to share the ice surface on the first day of each winter month but wanted a schedule that allowed each program to have the ice surface to themselves on other dates. Figure skating was granted ice surface every third day and hockey was granted the ice surface every fourth day. How many dates did each program have to themselves and how many did they have to share?

At the onset of the school fundraiser, the balance of the account was greater than $100. There were times, over the next eight transactions, during which the balance went up and down. What could each transaction have been and what is the current balance of the account?

~~~~~~

Ali's math course consisted of eight projects that contributed equally to the final grade. The course final grade was comprised only of these eight projects. On the initial project, Ali had their highest grade. What is the average grade for this student?

Within the problems students have opportunities to engage in mathematical discourse with peers.

Interestingly, when examining the rich tasks provided in the primary, elementary, and intermediate examples, you will notice that some may not be as connected to the lives of students out of school. But, all share opportunities for engagement and interest as well as a variety of approaches and representations to apply. Within the problems students have opportunities to engage in mathematical discourse with peers. It is through this engagement that learning can be extended regardless of where students are at in their understanding of mathematics.

As with open-ended problems, students have multiple points of entry and multiple points of exit when working through rich tasks. The presence of multiple points of entry and exit promotes student perseverance as they encounter stumbling blocks. When engaging with rich tasks, students move from a passive stance of *doing* mathematics to an active stance of *thinking* mathematically.

Like the other problem types we have seen throughout the chapter, rich tasks are comprised of the three characteristics found in problems: initial state, goal state, and obstacles. Much like open-ended problems, rich tasks offer flexibility in their approach and number of possibilities for a solution. Where there may be differences between the two problem types is that rich tasks promote a sense of relevancy for students that may not always be present in open-ended problems.

Progression of the Four Problem Types

The four common problem types have been demonstrated throughout the chapter. These are problems observed, applied, and/or discussed with teachers. In previous examples, the four problem types examined various concepts in primary, elementary, and intermediate grade levels. Now, one concept for each grade level band is highlighted to indicate what each problem type could be for a particular concept. This will show how each problem type can strengthen student learning while, at the same time, distinguish between the different thinking points amongst the four problem types.

A. Procedural

Determine the perimeter of a rectangle with a width of 3 cm and a length of 8 cm.

~~~~~~

B. Words-As-Labels

A farmer wanted to purchase fencing material for his rectangular field. The field was 70 m long and 40 m wide.

~~~~~~

C. Open-ended

The perimeter of a sign was between 80 cm and 100 cm. What could the length of the sides have been?

~~~~~~

D. Rich Tasks

The Grade 3 class was responsible for making the seasonal display in the school lobby. As part of this display, students had to decorate a bulletin board. The bulletin board had two sides that were much longer than the other two sides. Students wanted to place a decorative border around the bulletin board as it was the centerpiece of their display. What length of border will they need to go around the bulletin board?

A. Procedural

Solve: $185.49 \div 8$

~~~~~~

B. Words-As-Labels

David raised $185.49 when fundraising. He wanted to share the money equally between 8 charities. How much money will David donate to each charity?

~~~~~~

C. Open-ended

When dividing a decimal number by a single-digit whole number, the answer is between ten and twenty. What could the decimal number and single-digit whole number be?

~~~~~~

D. Rich Tasks

The local elementary school was fundraising to help four local charities. Although the students were hoping for a friendly whole number, the total money raised was a decimal number. If the students were hoping to share this money equally, how much money would each charity receive?

MULTIPLY FRACTIONS: INTERMEDIATE EXAMPLES

A. Procedural

Solve:
$\frac{1}{4} \times \frac{3}{5}$

~~~~~~

B. Words-As-Labels

The deck is $\frac{1}{4}$ the size of the garden. The garden is $\frac{3}{5}$ the size of the yard. What size is the deck in relation to the yard?

~~~~~~

C. Open-ended

When multiplying two factions, the product is less than 1 but greater than $\frac{1}{3}$. What could the two fractions be?

~~~~~~

D. Rich Tasks

The intermediate school's volleyball team had a busy schedule of games. During the first half of the season, the team won $\frac{1}{2}$ of the games. In the second half of the season, the team won $\frac{2}{3}$ of their games. How many games did the team win during the season?

While each of the four problem types have similarities, there are significant differences.

While each of the four problem types have similarities, there are significant differences. It is important, however, to note that students benefit from having experience in each type. Procedural problems allow students to focus on the process and to devote their energy to applying the process. It is a great exercise once students understand the concept. Words-as-labels problems provide students opportunities to engage with the concept and apply context to them. They can read the problem, determine the strategy to take, and then apply it to the concept. It is an additional layer of thinking for students. For open-ended problems, students have a greater degree of choice and are able to enter the problem from an accessibility point of view. Similarly, rich tasks provide opportunities for students to have choices but also provide the concept in a situation that relates to their lived experiences.

All four problem types play a part in student learning. It is an instructional decision when to assign such problem types and which problem types students will engage with most often. Guidance through this instructional decision is how students think mathematically as opposed to doing math by rote.

Defined Problems

The following is a visual highlighting the four problem types we have discussed.

The visual represents the typical problems assigned in the classroom that have been observed and worked on for many years. Each problem type falls under the defined problem category.

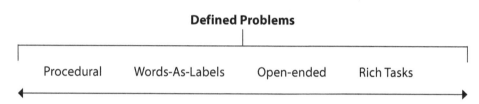

Each of the four problem types are examples of **defined problems**. As previously stated, defined problems include initial state, goal state, and obstacles. A central component of defined problems is that all the information students need to solve the problem is initially present (English, Fox, & Watters, 2005). While this may seem obvious to how all problems are structured, it is important to take a step back and reflect. Students are given a great deal of information and their ability to interpret has either been minimized or eliminated. Although the cognitive demand required to solve the problem increases as we move from left-to-right on the visual, students are still handed much, if not all, of the information necessary to overcome the obstacle and solve the problem.

Now, let's consider how often this happens in our everyday experiences outside of school. Very rarely are we handed all the information needed to overcome obstacles and solve the problem. Instead, we pause, interpret, and work through a situation to locate the information required to solve a problem. It is more of an active stance to learning.

So, in essence, if we are only providing students with defined problems, are we doing enough to move students from *doing* math to *thinking* mathematically?

So, in essence, if we are only providing students with defined problems, are we doing enough to move students from doing math to thinking mathematically?

Ill-Defined Problems

What I want to advocate is that we need to move further to the right if we want students *thinking* mathematically. The following visual shows the addition of ill-defined problems to the right-side.

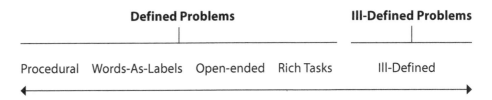

Ill-defined problems tend to be less common in the classroom but can be a game-changer for teachers wanting to reach their instructional goal of making mathematics relevant and having students *think mathematically*. One major distinction between defined problems and ill-defined problems is that ill-defined problems are missing one or more of the three characteristics of a problem: initial state, goal state, and obstacles. The purpose for missing one of more of these characteristics is to have problems that resemble ones that can be encountered in the real world.

Within ill-defined problems, the problem solver plays a significantly independent role. Typically, the initial state is vague and limited. Students must recognize that information is not as forthcoming as it usually is in defined problems. In addition, ill-defined problems rarely provide students with a specific goal state. Instead, the goal state is influenced and therefore determined by the problem solver. Within such a role, engagement is heightened as is the autonomy students have as they enter, work through, and solve the problem.

Let's consider the solution regarding ill-defined problems. While there are opportunities to have a range of solutions within defined problems (consider open-ended and rich tasks), there is an increased emphasis in the ability of students to arrive at a novel solution in ill-defined problems. As students have a more active presence in understanding the initial and goal state, there is greater variability in the possible solutions. This will then increase the likelihood for multiple paths toward solutions to exist.

There is the possibility to have multiple solutions in ill-defined problems because these problems tend to be complex and poorly defined. Solutions to ill-defined problems are based on the interpretations students make while working through a vague initial state and determining the goal state (Byun, Kwon, & Lee, 2014). What the student brings while interpreting the problem will shape whether their response makes sense or not. As such, you can see how students are autonomous and independent when engaging with ill-defined problems.

Ill-defined problems are unclear and require students to question what is known, what needs to be known, and how an accurate response to the problem can be achieved (Greenwald, 2000). Such ambiguity in the problem creates several pathways to multiple solutions. This multiplicity is influenced by the student's mathematical understanding and lived experiences. Therefore, instead of being the recipients of the information while working on defined problems, students become active, independent learners as they interpret vague situations and use their understanding and experiences to make meaning.

What the student brings while interpreting the problem will shape whether their response makes sense or not. As such, you can see how students are autonomous and independent when engaging with ill-defined problems.

The following are examples of ill-defined problems for Primary, Elementary, and Intermediate levels.

ILL-DEFINED PROBLEM: PRIMARY EXAMPLE

The Kindergarten classroom recognized that many of their supplies for centres were needing to be replaced. The teacher shared that they needed to buy new supplies but that they had a limited budget.

ILL-DEFINED PROBLEM: ELEMENTARY EXAMPLE

The local elementary school was selected as the site for the cross-county meet. As part of holding this meet, the school had to decide how to accommodate people wanting to watch the meet.

ILL-DEFINED PROBLEM: INTERMEDIATE EXAMPLE

In planning end-of-year activities, the school administration decide that the Grade 8 students would go on a field trip. The administration wanted to know what the cost per student would be for such a trip.

Ill-defined problems provide students with opportunities to engage in thinking mathematically instead of doing math. Ill-defined problems closely align to the problems students are faced with outside of the school setting.

Ill-defined problems provide students with opportunities to engage in *thinking* mathematically instead of *doing* math. Ill-defined problems closely align to the problems students are faced with outside of the school setting. Rarely outside of school do students encounter problems where all information is readily available and handed over to them. Instead, students need to examine the situation, interpret what is known and what is not known, and then take an active stance to working toward a possible solution. By engaging in ill-defined problems, students experience mathematics that resembles their lived experiences outside of school. They take an autonomous stance to their learning and work through obstacles that are similar to what they would need to work through to solve problems outside of school. It is about seeing math around them and applying such math to problems that they encounter. Ill-defined problems move students one step closer to being able to *think* mathematically.

Similarities and Differences between Defined Problems and Ill-Defined Problems

Throughout the chapter you have seen that there is a time and place for all problem types in the classroom. Each type of problem has a specific purpose. What we, as teachers, need to be aware of is the reasons we are choosing the problems we assign. To come to this conclusion we must understand the similarities and differences between defined problems and ill-defined problems.

The tables proceeding indicate the similarities and differences between defined and ill-defined problems. Let's examine the foundational aspects of each problem.

Three Characteristics of a Problem	
Defined	**Ill-Defined**
Clearly defined characteristics: • Initial state • Goal state • Obstacles	Missing one or more characteristics: • Initial state • Goal state • Obstacles

Open-ended	
Defined	**Ill-Defined**
• Not all defined problems are open-ended. • Procedural and words-as-labels are not open-ended. • Other examples of defined problems are open-ended.	All ill-defined problems are open-ended.

Rich Tasks	
Defined	**Ill-Defined**
• Procedural problems, words-as-labels problems, and some open-ended problems are not rich tasks. • Other defined problems, such as certain open-ended problems and rich tasks, fit these characteristics.	All ill-defined problems would be based within the characteristics of a rich task.

Multiple Strategy Options	
Defined	**Ill-Defined**
• Procedural problems only have one strategy option. • Words-as-labels may have multiple strategy options, but this is not a certainty. • Open-ended problems and rich tasks have multiple strategy solutions.	All ill-defined problems have multiple strategy options.

Multiple Solutions Available	
Defined	**Ill-Defined**
• Procedural problems and words-as-labels problems do not have multiple solutions available. • Open-ended problems have multiple solutions available. • Rich tasks may or may not have multiple solutions available.	All ill-defined problems have multiple solutions available.

Real World Context	
Defined	**Ill-Defined**
• Procedural problems and words-as-labels problems do not have real world context. • Open-ended problems may or may not have real world contexts. • Rich tasks may or may not have real world contexts.	All ill-defined problems has real world context.

Ill-defined problems are about students thinking mathematically instead of simply doing traditional math problems.

Each table shows the key differences between defined and ill-defined problems. For ill-defined problems, there is more ambiguity within the problem, creating multiple options for crafting a plan to overcome obstacles and for a solution. Such an approach to mathematical thinking allows for learning experiences in the classroom and everyday experiences outside of school to be more relevant. Ill-defined problems are about students *thinking* mathematically instead of simply *doing* traditional math problems. The thinking that students do when working through ill-defined problems is much more mathematized that the *doing* mathematics students do when working through defined problems.

Importance of Ill-Defined Problems

There are several advantages of assigning ill-defined problems in the classroom. We will explore these more in subsequent chapters but first let's understand why they are important. The following is a visual representation outlining the benefits of having students work through ill-defined problems.

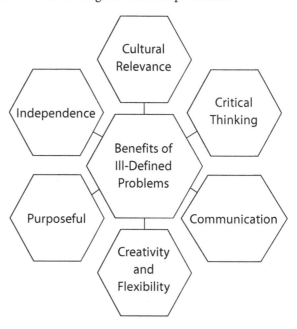

The visual identifies the benefits of having students work through ill-defined problems. Ill-defined problems are rooted in real-world experiences and, as such, present students with **culturally relevant** and meaningful problems.

Students must approach their work independently and use critical thinking skills. Students take an active learning stance to such problems in that they must generate aspects of the problem that provide structure. Students encounter a variety of stumbling blocks that require creativity and flexibility to solve the problem. And, with there being multiple points of entry and exit within ill-defined problems, students must be able to clearly communicate their thinking and the many steps they took to find a resolution.

Why Don't We See More Ill-defined Problems?

After hearing the benefits of assigning ill-defined problems in the classroom, you may be wondering why we don't see more ill-defined problems in the classroom. Consider the following comments made by teachers when asked why they don't use more ill-defined problems in the classroom.

THOUGHTS FROM PRIMARY TEACHERS

- "These types of problems are too hard for students. Students have difficulty with word problems. How can I expect them to have success with ill-defined problems?"
- "I can't imagine how you would go about assessing student work on ill-defined problems. There's just too many grey areas. How can I give students descriptive feedback if the problem is so open? It isn't just about if they are correct or not. But I would have to dig a lot deeper, and I am not sure what that would look like."

THOUGHTS FROM ELEMENTARY TEACHERS

- "I use the resource that I am directed to use. And in this resource, there are only defined problems. The problems are meant to support the learning of the unit. Students need this scaffold approach so that they can apply what they are seeing in the lesson. Plus, even if I want to do more ill-defined problems, where would I ever find them? I can't use something that I can't find."
- "My students take standardized tests, and I want them to do well on those tests. There are no ill-defined problems on any standardized test that I have ever given my students. So, why would I give them problems that they won't see again."

THOUGHTS FROM INTERMEDIATE TEACHERS

- "I try to show students how math is all around us. I can do this with word problems. I don't need ill-defined problems because they are just too much for students. I don't want students to be overwhelmed."
- "When students have standardized exams, they don't see ill-defined problems. They see defined problems. I want to provide opportunities for students to grow in their ability to solve problems that they will see later in the year. I want students to be able to experience success on problems that they need to do well on when taking standardized tests."

In considering the question of why we don't see more ill-defined problems in school, there are five underlying reasons:

1. Lack of Experience

Let's consider how many times we have been assigned an ill-defined problem while at school. Perhaps you found that there were none or very few ill-defined problems presented when you were the student. If we have had experiences of ill-defined problems it will likely be from when we were students in senior grade levels or postsecondary. Because of these experiences, we may have subconsciously attributed ill-defined problems to being something students work on in high school and/or college. However, we need to move away from this mindset. The benefits shared in the previous section can be applied to all students in Kindergarten through Grade 8, and we need to appreciate this.

2. Difficult to Create

Let's say that we do want to assign these problems in our Kindergarten through Grade 8 classrooms, now we have to find and/or create ill-defined problems. This can be challenging. There are more defined problems available to teachers than ill-defined problems. The lack of resources may hinder teachers from assigning them in the classroom. In terms of creating ill-defined problems, consider the complexity that may be involved. If we are not used to working with ill-defined problems and if we cannot find many to read through, the thought of creating some from scratch can be overwhelming.

3. Difficult to Assess

Now, let's say that we have an ill-defined problem ready to go, whether it is one we found or created. We have to consider how we are going to assess it. When assessing defined problems, there is less ambiguity because there is less openness. Traditionally, there is one solution and one or a few strategy options available to arrive at the solution. This is not the case for ill-defined problems. There is openness in the interpretation of the problem, in the plans that students can create to lead to one of many possible solutions. What this openness does is move assessment from being about following a prescribed approach to being flexible, fluid, and responsive. As teachers, we must appreciate this openness in student thinking and be able to account for it whether it is through conversation, observation, and/or product.

4. Standardized Tests

Think back to the standardized tests that you have seen in the past or the standardized tests that you have seen recently. Many, if not all the problems are defined. There are a variety of defined problems (procedural, words-as-labels, open-ended, rich tasks), but there are little to no ill-defined problems. When teachers observe that standardized tests do not contain ill-defined problems, they may be less motivated to offer these in class. Teachers want their students to do their best on the standardized tests and as such, focus on problem types that they will encounter on such tests. As a result, we see few ill-defined problems in the classroom.

5. Moving from Product to Process

Ill-defined problems enable students to mathematize their thinking and to become capable and confident math learners. Moving from product to process highlights the intricacies in student thinking and moves learning from being teacher-directed to student-led.

When considering openness, we must consider how moving from defined problems to ill-defined problems moves the focus of mathematics from product to process, and from *doing* mathematics to *thinking mathematically*. Ill-defined problems enable students to mathematize their thinking and to become capable and confident math learners. Moving from product to process highlights the intricacies in student thinking and moves learning from being teacher-directed to student-led.

As can be seen from the teachers' comments there are similarities as to why they do not assign ill-defined problems in the classroom. However, what we are doing is removing one category of problems from students' mathematical experiences. Removing this category means we are eliminating any opportunity to strengthen students' ability to work through ill-defined problems. Students' mathematical thinking is restricted when they are given problems that come with all the needed information to solve the problem. This lessens students' autonomy and independence as mathematicians. When we remove ill-defined problems from the classroom, we increase the isolation of mathematics from the everyday experiences' students have outside of school.

Summary

We hear countless references to problems when talking about mathematics. However, it is important to take the time to consider the perspectives of different problems. Problems are characterized by three aspects: initial state, goal state, and obstacles. When examining the problems assigned in many classrooms, it is mostly defined problems that students encounter. While there is a range within defined problems—procedural problems to rich tasks—all the information required to solve the problem is provided. These are not problems we encounter in the real world.

As educators we need to consider and offer students more experiences and working with ill-defined problems will do this. Within such problems, students encounter messy situations that reflect everyday experiences. There are benefits to assigning ill-defined problems, so let's make the switch.

CHAPTER 2

Understanding the Different Ways to Problem Solve

Students need to learn how to *think* mathematically instead of simply *doing* math. Students can apply formulaic processes to solve mathematical problems without question. And, when they hit a stumbling block, they are unable to work through it. Many students just go through the motions, doing math by rote. This is not enough. Students should be able to make sense of the problems and the math required to solve these problems. Students should be capable and confident math learners. First, teachers need to be cognizant of the types of problems students are tackling. Then they must explain the purpose of problems to their students.

Thinking mathematically is inherent in problem solving. Problem solving requires the student to approach a problem, regardless of the type, from the meaning-making perspective. Students are to frame, support, and consolidate their understanding as they navigate the problem and reach a conclusion. As such, we need to support students in becoming problem solvers. However, before we jump to this, we need to pause and consider what we mean by problem solving. Without a clear comprehension of problem solving how we can ensure we are creating tasks that will encourage students to problem solve and deal with stumbling blocks.

Defining Problem Solving

Consider the following responses from teachers when they were asked to define problem solving.

PRIMARY EXAMPLE: A TEACHER EXPLAINS

Problem solving requires students to pause and consider what the problem is asking. It means that they don't have an immediate understanding of the problem or a plan to solve the problem. They really struggle.

ELEMENTARY EXAMPLE: A TEACHER EXPLAINS

When I think of problem solving, I think of the strategies that students need to apply to solve a novel problem. Do students have the necessary tools to approach the problem and solve it? It is about students having to think about what is given in the problem and deciding on how to use this information to get to the solution.

INTERMEDIATE EXAMPLE: A TEACHER EXPLAINS

Problem solving is the process of applying what you know in new and unique ways to tackle problems you haven't already encountered.

Each of the teachers' comments reference the task that students are assigned. Each teacher stresses that when students are presented with a problem there is an initial state of uncertainty of how to get to the end goal. If we recall our definition of problems from Chapter 1, we can see that teachers are describing the obstacles students encounter when moving from the initial state to the goal state. The teachers are referring to defined problems when defining problem solving.

Now, let's consider how students respond when asked to define problem solving.

PRIMARY EXAMPLE: A STUDENT EXPLAINS

Problem solving is when you have to work to find an answer to a problem. It can't be for easy problems. It has to be for hard problems.

ELEMENTARY EXAMPLE: A STUDENT EXPLAINS

My teacher talks a lot about productive struggle. Problem solving is when we have to work through stumbling blocks to find an answer. We don't know how to do it right away, but we figure it out.

INTERMEDIATE EXAMPLE: A STUDENT EXPLAINS

Problem solving is about using different strategies to solve problems. It is different than practice. In practice, we immediately know what to do to solve a problem and we do it. When we problem solve, we have to figure out how to move from the information we are given to finding the answer to the question being asked in the problem.

The students all refer to a greater level of difficulty when problem solving. They each comment on having to *work* to find the answer to a problem. This *work* can be thought of as productive struggle and the obstacles that students must overcome in reaching the answer (goal state). By referencing this work students made a distinction between easily finding the solution to having to work through stumbling blocks to find the answer. Problem solving involves effort.

When examining the comments from both teachers and students, there are significant similarities. Both categories highlight how problem solving requires effort in working through the problem. This effort results from a state of the unknown being present in the task assigned to students. This unknown comes from not having a plan to immediately move from the initial state to the goal state.

Let's take a step back and consider how problem solving requires effort. This effort is rooted in a state of unknown. The unknown requires students to weigh the various points of information in a problem and how this information will lead them to choosing an approach that will lead them toward a meaningful response. Therefore, problem solving should be thought of as a verb. The thinking and processes students engage with while identifying the state of unknown is the action taken in dealing with the obstacles.

When we approach problem solving as a thinking process, or as a verb, we turn our attention to the thinking that students are engaged within. We can then recognize and appreciate the many emotional states our students experience as they problem solve. Students must persevere when problem solving as they will undoubtedly encounter stumbling blocks not knowing how to respond. During this perseverance, students engage in self-talk. They talk themselves through the process and use this self-monitoring strategy to assist in meaning-making. It is imperative that students demonstrate a growth mindset. As students try different strategies not all approaches will be successful so we want students to take on the perspective that they can learn from their experiences and use them to make more informed decisions.

When approaching problem solving from a thinking process we can appreciate the complexity involved. Consider the following **cognitive processes** that would be represented within problem solving.

- Students are presented with a task:
  - If the task does not provide cognitive dissonance, then it is an *opportunity for practice*, not problem solving. If the task does provide students with cognitive dissonance, then it is an *opportunity for problem solving*.
- When problem solving, students must
  - Understand the problem (the initial state)
    - Students utilize cognitive strategies to accurately understand the problem.
  - Recognize the goal state
    - Cognitive strategies are utilized by the student to recognize the end goal.
  - Decide on a strategy that leads them from the initial state to the goal state
  - Enact the strategy
    - Self-monitor when enacting the strategy.
    - Determine if the strategy is leading to a solution.
    - Overcome stumbling blocks.
  - Determine if the strategy leads to a meaningful response
    - If it did, review the work.
    - If it did not, consider alternative strategies.

When we approach problem solving as a thinking process, or as a verb, we turn our attention to the thinking that students are engaged within. We can then recognize and appreciate the many emotional states our students experience as they problem solve.

Problem solving is multifaceted. Problem solving has various stages. At each stage, we want students to think confidently and apply their mathematical understanding toward solving problems.

The Problem Solving Stages

When problem solving students are engaged in a range of thinking processes. The work of George Polya (2004) has been used to identify the key thinking points within the problem-solving process. Polya referred to this as the four principles of problem solving. Some people who have taken up his work refer to the principles as steps, while others refer to the principles as stages. For the purposes of this book, we will refer to Polya's four principles as the four problem solving stages.

Each stage of problem solving is layered. A single stage is comprised of different thinking points in the decision-making process. I am providing an overview of the stages but each stage is quite in-depth and can engage students in significant thinking. There can be productive struggle within each stage and the student must rely on their thinking to move through the stages.

Using the work of Polya (2004), the following are the accepted four stages of problem solving:

1. Understanding the problem
2. Crafting a plan
3. Carrying out the plan
4. Reviewing your work

Understanding the Problem

When aiming to understand the problem its significance can be overlooked. Many times, regardless of the grade level, students will read a problem and jump into a decided strategy. By doing this, students run the risk of not fully understanding the problem. And, without fully understanding the problem, how can students approach their work from a meaning-making lens? How will they be able to self-monitor their thinking and determine if their work is making sense when solving the problem?

When presented with a problem, students should be able to clearly articulate what the problem is asking. They should be able to restate the problem and determine if there is enough information given to plan a strategy that would solve the problem. Once the problem is rephrased in their own words, the student can understand the problem from an overall perspective. The thinking process begins during the restating phase. Students must read the problem, process it, and then reframe it so that they can clearly understand its overall meaning. Too often, this first stage of problem solving seems like it is slowing down students from the real work of enacting a plan. However, without a firm understanding of the problem, the foundation for their work is fragile and not supported with understanding.

When presented with a problem, students should be able to clearly articulate what the problem is asking. They should be able to restate the problem and determine if there is enough information given to plan a strategy that would solve the problem.

Crafting a Plan

An analytic approach is required to weigh the strengths and weaknesses of each possible plan.

Crafting a plan can be overwhelming. After the student understands the problem, a plan must be crafted so that they can work through the obstacles to reach the goal state. It may seem like a simple step, choosing a plan, but there are many thinking points within this step. First, the student must reflect on their understanding of the problem and identify a plan that can be applied to the information given to support them in reaching the goal state. In crafting this plan, the student must select from a range of possibilities. An analytic approach is required to weigh the strengths and weaknesses of each possible plan. Then identify the best option for solving the problem.

During the second stage of problem solving it is common that students will become frustrated when selecting a plan. This is caused by two factors. First, the student could be overwhelmed with the problem and not be sure which plan would best align to solving it. Perhaps the student is struggling to select a plan from a few options. Second, the student could be struggling to identify any plan that will solve the problem. Whether the struggle is selecting the right plan from several options or in identifying one plan, the second stage of problem solving is significant. It is throughout this stage that students must constantly go back to their understanding of the problem and generate a plan that is consistent with what the problem is asking.

Carrying out the Plan

Carrying out the plan is when students apply the plan that they crafted. During the third stage students must execute their plan and bring it to completion. This completion can take one of two forms. First, the completion could be that the plan is carried out without error. The student has arrived at the best response for the question being asked and it makes sense to the context provided within the problem. Second, the completion could be that the plan is carried out and the student realizes that it is not leading to a response that addresses the question or that it does not make sense. When this occurs, the student must go back to the first stage of problem solving and see if their understanding of the problem is accurate. This will allow the student to select a new plan and carry it out with the hope of solving the problem.

All too often, carrying out the plan is seen as the heart of problem solving. It is viewed by students as being the work of problem solving. However, this is an oversimplification of what problem solving entails. Carrying out the plan only happens after students understand the problem and have decided on a plan that will lead them toward a solution. Carrying out the plan is important and requires students to self-monitor their thinking, but students should be self-monitoring their thinking throughout the first two stages of problem solving. It is important, in this third stage, that students recognize their plan is suitable in reaching a solution to the problem, their work is accurate, they carried out the plan well, and solved the problem. If not, they need to go back to the drawing board.

Reviewing Your Work

Reviewing your work enables students to reflect on the problem and their work. It is during this stage that the student can take a step back and examine their work with a big picture lens. Students can analyze their understanding of the problem and whether it was accurate, whether the plan they selected was the most suitable one they could have chosen, what worked best in their problem-solving process and what areas could be strengthened the next time they engage with a problem. It is the thinking that occurs within this stage of problem solving that summarizes and synthesizes their experience. It approaches the problem-solving experience from a macro level so that students can see beyond the individual thinking points to seeing how it all comes together. During this stage, students can reflect on their problem-solving experience to assist them in solving problems they will encounter in the future.

While this stage of problem solving is mainly a reflective thinking approach, it cannot be omitted or rushed through.

While this stage of problem solving is mainly a reflective thinking approach, it cannot be omitted or rushed through. The thinking that occurs within this stage is as important as when working through the previous stages. Each stage highlights significant thinking points within the problem-solving experience and each stage interweaves with the others. Problem solving is not a linear process. Problem solving is a fluid process by which the student engages in an iterative process.

Problem Solving Stages in Action

Each stage of problem solving is important. It is imperative that students, and teachers, recognize that one part is not more important than another. Close attention should be paid to the purpose of each stage. Providing an overview of each stage, however, is not enough. We, as educators, must be mindful that problem solving is an iterative process that involves the revision of thinking and clarifying of one's thoughts.

Consider when educators share the stages with students without highlighting the iterative nature of problem solving.

When viewing problem solving as four separate stages, we run the risk of positioning problem solving as a linear process. And, in doing so, students may view problem solving to be a step-by-step process.

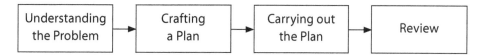

The visual oversimplifies problem solving. It implies students move through each stage and that success occurs in a step-by-step manner. This is not true. Problem solving is messy. Students will enter a one stage of problem solving only to return to a previous stage. For example, once you craft a plan and carry it out, you realize that it is not leading you toward the solution. You need to pause, go back, and clarify your understanding of the problem and possibly craft a new plan. This can happen multiple times. Another example is that once you review your work, you recognize that you did not address the question within the problem and that you are missing information. You may have to go all the way back to the first stage—understanding the problem—and work through the problem again. Problem solving is an iterative process that students engage in. Consider the visual below and how fluid it is.

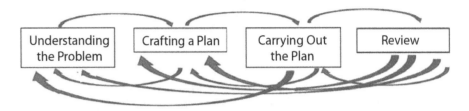

Take a moment to compare the visual with the interconnectivity of the arrows to the visual that has just one arrow between each of the stages. You will notice how there is much more complexity within the second visual. This is what we want students to realize that problem solving encompasses. It is about continuously clarifying and revising our thinking. As one student put it years ago, problem solving is about going back to the drawing board to better understand the problem and knowing how to work through it.

The following are teachers' comments, stemming from observations they have made of the four stages of problem solving from the perspective of instruction and student learning.

PRIMARY EXAMPLE: A TEACHER EXPLAINS

Instruction

I am not sure if I do the four stages justice. I address each of the stages, but I tend to run out of time when we get to the end of the lesson. What this means is that I don't do much with the last step of reviewing work.

Student Learning

Students seem to want to get right into solving the problem. Most times, they will read the problem one time and then decide on a strategy. If that strategy doesn't work, they will think of another. Students don't seem interested in understanding their thinking or considering other ways to solve the problem.

ELEMENTARY EXAMPLE: A TEACHER EXPLAINS

Instruction

I think it is important to highlight and emphasize each of the four stages. I have found that students don't want to spend much time on understanding the problem or reviewing. So, what I do, is show how important these stages are. For understanding the problem, I stress how if we don't understand what is being asked then we can't know if we have solved the problem. And, for reviewing, I tell students that if we don't look back at our work how are we to know if we can do it better next time.

Student Learning

My students do not like to go *backwards* in terms of the stages. What I mean is that if they are carrying out the plan and if they recognize that the plan is not working, they just give up. They don't want to go back and clarify their understanding of the problem or go back and consider a new plan. When I ask them why, my students say that this means that they are wrong and can't solve the problem. They are not seeing how fluid problem solving is. Instead, they think of it as a linear step 1, step 2, step 3, step 4, finish.

INTERMEDIATE EXAMPLE: A TEACHER EXPLAINS

Instruction

In terms of instruction, I really don't spend a lot of time working on the four stages. I assume that students understand and can apply each of the strategies. Instead, what I do focus on is providing the time for students to share their thinking at the end of the problem and sharing which plan they used to arrive at the solution. So, I guess, I do spend time on one of the stages more than others—the reviewing stage.

Student Learning

By the time students get to me, I am hoping that they already have proficiency with the problem solving stages. Instead, I find that I have to really help them consider multiple plans to attack the problem. I need to support them in having a toolbox of strategies available so that if plan A doesn't work, that they have a plan B. I need them to persevere.

Looking at the comments it is evident that there is a shift in thinking from primary through intermediate grade levels. While each of the stages play a pivotal role in problem solving, the teachers' comments highlight that there is not always equal weight given to the stages. As a result of this, students may come to appreciate one aspect of problem solving as being more important than others and thereby jeopardize their ability to problem solve. There is a lack of appreciation in understanding how complex problem solving can be and how each stage interweaves with one another. The comments also speak to student learning. Students are not approaching problem solving as an iterative process that requires the students to continuously question and revise their thinking.

The following are students' comments about their thoughts and experiences with problem solving, especially the four stages of problem solving.

PRIMARY EXAMPLE: A STUDENT EXPLAINS

It can be hard to understand the problem. When I ask for help, the teacher gets me to read the problem again. I try to read the problem three times. But, it usually doesn't help. I don't know what the problem is about or what I need to do.

I am pretty good at problem solving. The one part that I think I don't need to do all the time is the review part. Really, reviewing is just double checking my work to see if I did the plan the right way. But, even when I review my work and see that I have done everything right, my answer isn't always right. How come this happens? If review means double check, and if I don't find anything wrong in my calculations, how come my answer isn't right? Am I reviewing the wrong way?

I can usually do all the stages the way I am supposed to. The one thing I find hard is when my plan doesn't work, I have to think of another plan. It is hard enough to find one plan. When something doesn't work, I'm stuck. There's nothing to do.

The students, no matter the grade level, are all indicating a problem with understanding the problem-solving process. The primary student is having trouble with the first stage (understanding the problem). The elementary student finds the fourth stage (reviewing) difficult. The intermediate student is unable to understand what to do at the second stage (crafting a plan) or finding an alternate plan if their first choice doesn't yield the solution. Clearly, the students have misconceptions about the four stages and the strategies that are required for each. More specifically, students are not seeing the true meaning of each phase and how the phases are support one another. For example, the primary student is struggling with strategies to understand the whole problem. The elementary student is not fully aware of how reviewing is more than double checking calculations. It is about looking at our work from an overall perspective and determining its meaning and how it can be supportive of future problem-solving experiences. The intermediate student is not recognizing that crafting a plan is largely influenced by understanding the problem, and if the student is struggling with crafting a plan there is a question as to whether they really understand the problem.

Therefore, both teacher and student comments demonstrate that more work can be done with problem solving and how the four stages are an iterative process. It is not a one-and-done process. Instead, it is a thinking process that requires clarification and revision.

To support students in understanding and applying the four stages of problem solving, consider the following graphic organizer.

Both teacher and student comments demonstrate that more work can be done with problem solving and how the four stages are an iterative process. It is not a one-and-done process. Instead, it is a thinking process that requires clarification and revision.

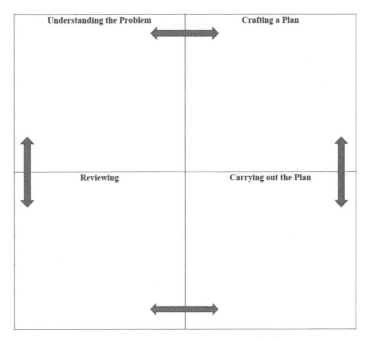

Within this graphic organizer, students are provided spaces to record their thinking for each of the four stages of problem solving. The organizer approaches the stages within a clockwise formation. It starts with understanding the problem. The arrows I have included in this graphic organizer indicate when students can return to a previous box (stage) if necessary. The arrows highlight the fluidity within the problem-solving process. The graphic organizer works to illustrate how problem solving is an iterative process.

In the past, I have encouraged students to record a few words, up to one sentence, next to the arrows to indicate if they are moving forward or if they return to a previous stage. The point of recording their thinking is to clarify the problem-solving process for students, support them in communicating their understanding, and provide more data for teachers to assess student learning.

Now let's consider the graphic organizer below.

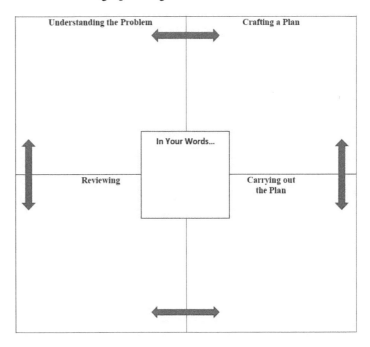

In this graphic organizer, I add a box at the centre for students to record the problems in their own words. It is an attempt to have students take the time and consider what the problem is asking. It is similar, but not the same as the first stage of problem solving (understanding the problem). "In Your Words…" requires the students to take a step back and restate the problem in a way that makes sense to them. Through paraphrasing the problem, students must read it and process it. This additional step is meant to strengthen the understanding of the problem.

Both graphic organizers are meant to support students in strengthening their ability to address each phase of the problem-solving process as well as their ability to navigate these stages throughout the process. It is imperative that students recognize the necessity to be able to go back and forth through these stages as they navigate the problem. By including the arrows, students are required to document their thinking as to why they are moving forward in the stages or why they have decided to return to a previous stage. It is through this metacognitive activity that students become confident and capable math learners. They move from doing math to thinking mathematically.

Problem Solving and Classroom Connections

As previously stated, I have encountered a continuum of problems in classrooms and through conversations with other educators. Consider the visual below.

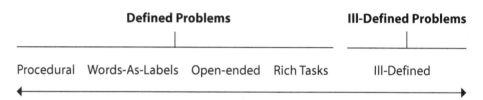

The visual shows that there are two categories of problems: defined and ill-defined. Recall that defined problems consist of three characteristics: initial state, goal state, and obstacles (Greenwald, 2000). While these three characteristics are present, a unifying aspect of defined problems is that all the information students need to solve the problem is initially present (English, Fox & Watters, 2005).

As previously shared, the most common type of problem that I have observed in Kindergarten through Grade 8 classrooms are defined problems. For this reason, I will focus on highlighting and demonstrating the four problem solving stages in the work of students solving defined problems. I will do this for words-as-labels, open-ended, and rich tasks problem types. There will be work samples for primary, elementary, and intermediate levels.

Problem Solving Stages in Words-As-Labels

Student work samples for primary, elementary, and intermediate levels are explored at each of the problem-solving stages. I will use one of the graphic organizers discussed earlier in the chapter so there is a clear depiction and understanding of the student thinking reported during each stage.

The following problem was assigned to primary students. As you can see in this problem there is no extraneous information provided.

> *Winnie had three fish in the fish tank. Winnie's family bought her more fish for her birthday. Now, there are nine fish in Winnie's fish tank. How many fish did Winnie's family buy her?*

Let's explore the work sample from a primary student.

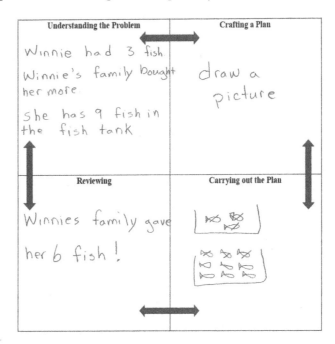

The primary student's work sample identified the important information within the problem. Once the information was recorded the student decided to draw a picture to work through the problem. For this picture, the student created two fish tanks—one with the three fish, where the problem started; the other fish tank with the nine fish, where the problem ends. In carrying out the plan the student crossed off three fish in the first tank and three in the second tank, to indicate that these three were not included in what Winnie's family purchased for her in the problem. Then, in reviewing the work, the student wrote a concluding sentence.

You can see that this problem involved an initial state, three fish, and the goal state, nine fish. The obstacle was to determine how many fish were purchased to move from three to nine.

Elementary

The following problem was assigned to elementary students. As you will see in this problem, the reference to 20 soccer balls is extraneous information.

Josef's class set a goal to raise enough money to purchase 20 soccer balls for the school. Josef's class had twenty-eight students. Each student raised $50. How much money did Josef's class raise for the fundraiser?

Let's explore the work sample from an elementary student.

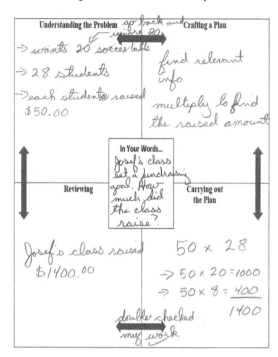

The work sample starts with the student going through the problem-solving process and first paraphrasing the problem in their own words. The student listed information contained within the problem in the first stage, understanding the problem. Next, in crafting the plan stage, the student decides to work with the relevant information. This decision means the student can cross out the reference to the 20 soccer balls since it is irrelevant to solving the problem. In the final two stages, carrying out the plan and reviewing, the student indicates that they double-checked their work as a form of review.

For this problem, the initial state was fundraising to purchase 20 soccer balls. The 28 students in the class each raised $50. So, the goal state was to identify the amount of money the class raised. The obstacles for the student to overcome was to craft a plan and then carry it out.

Intermediate

The following problem was assigned to intermediate students.

Two friends decided to share a pizza. Ethan ate $\frac{2}{5}$ of the pizza and Elias at $\frac{2}{4}$ of the pizza. How much of the pizza wasn't eaten?

Let's explore the work sample from an intermediate student.

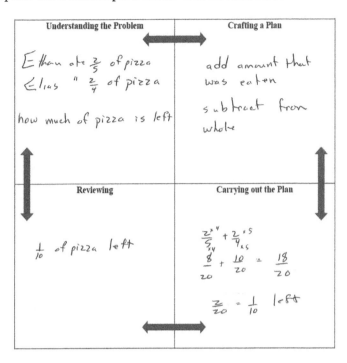

The work sample begins with the student following the problem-solving process by listing the relevant information as well as the question. Next, when working in crafting the plan stage, the student indicates that they would have to add the amounts of pizza each person ate and then subtract that amount from the whole to determine how much of the pizza was left. In carrying out the plan, the student used common denominators to add, and then wrote that two-twentieths, of one-tenth, was left. During the reviewing stage of problem solving, the student records a sentence to indicate that they solved the problem by answering the question.

The initial state consisted of two friends eating some pizza. The goal state was to identify the amount of the pizza left after the two friends finished eating. The obstacle was to determine how to find out how much pizza remained. For this, the student had to first find the total amount eaten and then subtract this amount from the whole.

Problem Solving Stages in Open-ended Problems

Student work samples for primary, elementary, and intermediate levels are explored at each of the problem-solving stages. I will use one of the graphic organizers discussed earlier in the chapter so there is a clear depiction and understanding of the student thinking reported during each stage.

Primary

The following problem was assigned to primary students:

A pattern has more green cubes than red cubes. What could the pattern look like?

Let's explore the work sample from a primary student.

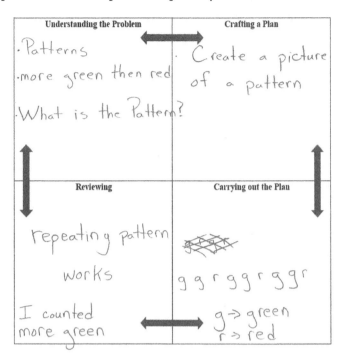

The work sample begins with the student identifying that the problem is about patterns. There are more green than red cubes, and it is necessary to determine the pattern being referenced. Next, when crafting a plan, the student indicates that drawing a picture can be used to work through the problem. In carrying out the plan, the student uses letters representing the red and green cubes (g is for green, r is for red). First, the student starts with a repeating pattern of one of each elements (one green, one red). But the student discards this pattern and crafts another.

The initial state is stating that a pattern consisting of more green than red cubes is needed. The goal state identifies the pattern. The obstacle was to determine a pattern that fit the restrictions.

Elementary

The following problem was assigned to elementary students:

> Consider four numbers that are greater than 10 000 but less than 100 000. The sum of the digits in each number is 21. Arrange the four numbers in ascending order.

Let's explore the work sample from an elementary student.

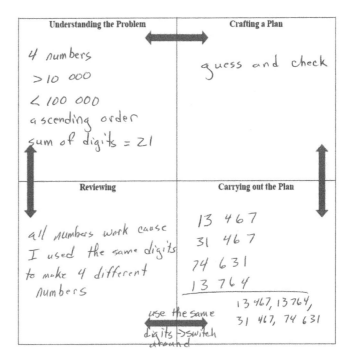

The work sample begins with the student listing information found in the problem. Next, the student decides to apply a "guess and check" approach to solving the problem. When carrying out the plan of "guess and check," the student identifies that once the first number matches the criteria (greater than 10 000, less than 100 000, the sum of the digits is 21), they create three other numbers using the same digits but in different order. Within the final two stages, the student reviews their work by repeating their plan involving the same five digits in a different order.

In this problem, the initial state is to identify four numbers that meet the criteria. The goal state arranges these numbers in ascending order. The obstacle is that the four numbers must follow the criteria established within the problem.

Intermediate

The following problem was assigned to intermediate students:

> When solving an equation, I determine that the value of x is 4. What could the equation be?

Let's explore the work sample from an intermediate student.

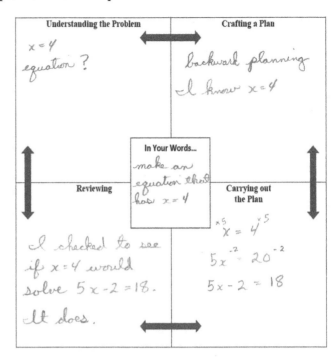

The work sample begins with the student paraphrasing the problem in their own words. The student lists the information found in the problem in the first stage of problem solving. Next, when working in the crafting the plan stage, the student decides to apply a backwards design approach to problem solving. From this decision, the student then starts with x = 4, and carries out operations (e.g., multiplication, subtraction) to develop an equation. When reviewing their work, the student inputs 4 as the value of x, and is able to solve the equation.

In this problem, the initial state was identifying an equation to address the goal state of x = 4. The obstacle was to move from the initial state to the goal state. To identify an equation that met the criteria of x = 4 meant the student had to engage in problem solving.

Problem Solving Stages in Rich Tasks

Student work samples for primary, elementary, and intermediate levels are explored at each of the problem-solving stages. I will use one of the graphic organizers discussed earlier in the chapter so there is a clear depiction and understanding of the student thinking reported during each stage.

Primary

The following problem was assigned to primary students:

> Two students were using cube-a-links to make a pattern. One student was making a repeating pattern while the other student was making an increasing pattern. When working on their individual patterns, the students realized that they used the same colored cube-a-link for the tenth item in their patterns. Is there a way that they will use the same color again for the twelfth item in their patterns?

Let's explore the work sample from a primary student.

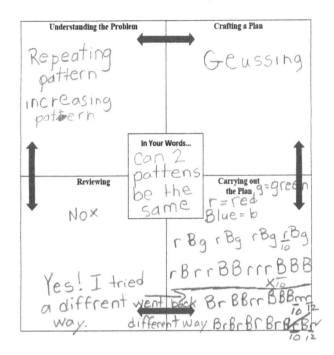

The work sample begins with the student paraphrasing the problem in their own words. The focus of this problem is to determine if the two different patterns each have the same color for the twelfth item in the pattern as it did for the tenth. The student lists the two types of patterns in understanding the problem: repeating patterns and increasing patterns. Next, the student decides to apply a guess approach to solving the problem. Initially, the student determines that the two patterns do not have the same color for the tenth item. The student then answered no in the reviewing stage but returned to carry out the plan again using a different arrangement of colors. This return provided the student with the correct response and they communicate this in the reviewing stage. Note that the student writes a brief note on the arrow between the carrying out the plan and reviewing stages to indicate that they returned to try solving the problem again.

In this problem, the initial state was two patterns with the same color for the tenth element. The goal state was to determine if there existed a way that the two patterns would have the same color for the twelfth item. The obstacle was determining if this was possible.

Elementary

The following problem was assigned to elementary students:

> The school soccer team decided to purchase team hoodies. These hoodies were $22 each or 4 for $80. If there were 22 players on the team, how much money would the hoodies cost?

Let's explore the work sample from an elementary student.

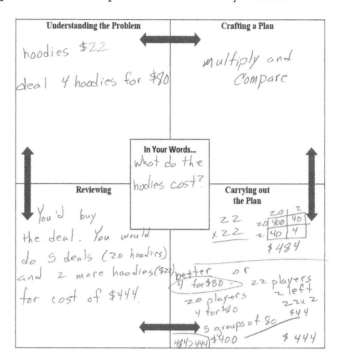

The elementary student starts by paraphrasing the problem. The paraphrasing is brief since it only references the question. The focus in this problem is to determine the cost of the 22 hoodies. The student lists the price per hoodie and the deal if four hoodies are purchased. Next, the student decides to multiply the number of hoodies by the price, at the deal and non-deal prices. Then, the student compares the cost to determine the better deal. The student determines using the deal will cost $444 and the non-deal will $484. The student then compares the two costs to determine that using the price of four hoodies is the best deal. Within the reviewing stage, the student provides a detailed account of their work.

In this problem, the student is given two costs for the hoodies that depends on whether the hoodies were purchased individually or in groups of four. The goal state is to determine the cost of the hoodies. To overcome the obstacle, the student had to decide on how to purchase the hoodies, deal or non-deal price, and find the total cost.

Intermediate

The problem below was assigned to intermediate students:

> At the onset of the school fundraiser, the balance of the account was greater than $100. There were times, over the next eight transactions, during which the balance went up and down. What could each transaction have been and what is the current balance of the account?

Let's explore the work sample from an intermediate student.

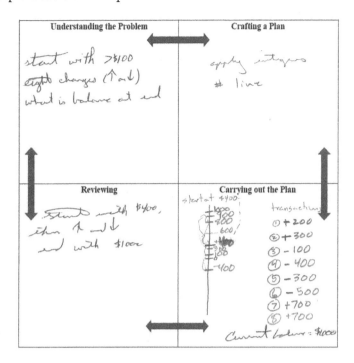

The intermediate student lists the relevant information within the problem to demonstrate their understanding. From here, the student crafts a plan that involved integers and a number line. When carrying out the plan, the student records deposits as positive integers and withdrawals as negative integers. The student starts with an initial balance of $400, and then uses the number line to indicate changes to the amount within the account. At the reviewing stage, the student references their approach and indicated the final balance of $1000 in the account.

In this problem, the initial state is that students are directed to the balance of the account as greater than $100. From this, there are eight transactions. The goal state determines the final balance in the account. The obstacle is determining the amount within each of the eight transactions and then finding the end balance.

Problem Solving and Ill-Defined Problems

In comparison to defined problems, ill-defined problems are missing one or more of the characteristics of a problem: initial state, goal state, and/or obstacles. In missing one of more of the characteristics, ill-defined problems closely resemble problems that we encounter in everyday life.

Next, I will focus on highlighting and demonstrating the four problem solving stages within the work of students when solving ill-defined problems. The work samples represent the techniques used by primary, elementary, and intermediate students.

Problem Solving Stages in Ill-Defined Problems

Student work samples for primary, elementary, and intermediate levels are explored at each of the problem-solving stages. I will use one of the graphic organizers discussed earlier in the chapter so there is a clear understanding of how the four stages of problem solving relate to solving ill-defined problems.

Primary

The following problem was assigned to primary students.

> *The Kindergarten classroom recognized that many of their supplies for centres were needing to be replaced. The teacher shared that they needed to buy new supplies but that they had a limited budget.*

Let's explore the work sample from a primary student.

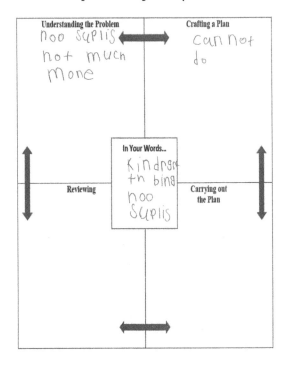

The primary student starts the problem-solving process by paraphrasing the problem. The paraphrase references that the Kindergarten class needs to buy new supplies. Next, the student lists two important pieces of information; new supplies and not much money. However, the primary student is unable to craft a plan for the problem as they did not have enough information to make an informed choice. The student does not list any work in either the carrying out the plan or reviewing stage.

In this problem, the initial state informs students that the Kindergarten classroom needs new supplies. However, in determining the goal state, there is not a description of what supplies are needed or how much money is allocated to purchase the supplies. Without this information, the students will not be aware of the restrictions contained within the obstacles. As such, the three characteristics of a problem are not present.

Elementary

The following problem was assigned to elementary students.

> *The local elementary school was selected as the site for the cross-country meet. As part of holding this meet, the school had to decide how to accommodate people wanting to watch the meet.*

Let's explore the work sample from an elementary student.

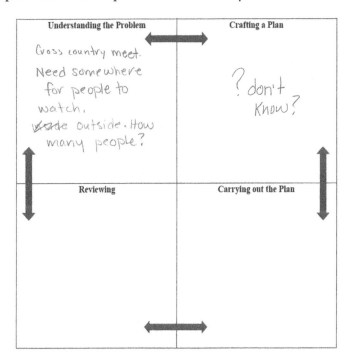

The elementary student starts the problem-solving process by listing important information. This information includes there is a cross-country meet and the need for a location for spectators. However, the student is unable to list how many people are expected to be in the audience. From this, the student records a question mark and the phrase "don't know" into the crafting a plan stage. Without this information, the student is unable to craft and carry out a plan. There is no need to review any work because the student cannot identify enough information within the problem to work toward a solution.

In this problem, the initial state includes a reference to a cross-country meet and the need to accommodate the spectators. However, in determining the goal state, there is no information given as to how many people will attend. Without this numerical data, the students are not aware of the restrictions contained within the obstacles. As such, the three characteristics of a problem are not present.

Intermediate

The following problem was assigned to intermediate students.

> *In planning end-of-year activities, the school administration decided that the Grade 8 students would go on a field trip. The administration wanted to know what the cost per student would be for such a trip.*

Let's explore the work sample from an intermediate student.

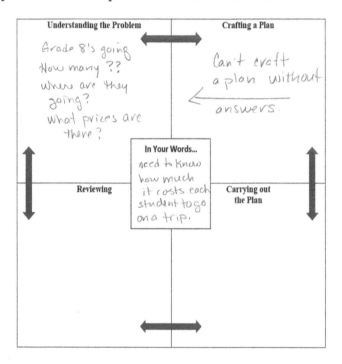

The intermediate student starts the problem-solving process by paraphrasing the original problem as needing to know how much it would cost each student to go on a field trip. From this paraphrasing, the student lists the relevant information as Grade 8 students, but also indicates that there are questions as to how many students will attend, the location of the trip, and the associated prices. The student then states that they cannot craft a plan without knowing the answers to these questions. That is as much of the graphic organizer the student can complete.

In this problem, the initial state includes a reference to the school administration wanting to send their Grade 8 students on a field trip. However, in determining the goal state, there is no information given regarding the destination, associated prices, and number students who will attend. Without this numerical data, the students are not be aware of the restrictions contained within the obstacles. As such, the three characteristics of a problem are not present.

Consider the following comments made by teachers regarding the inefficiency of the above graphic organizers and Polya's problem solving stages when students encounter ill-defined problems.

I was hesitant to assign ill-defined problems at first. I thought it was too ambiguous. However, I must admit that my students loved it. They loved that they could add their thoughts and information to it. I saw lots of engagement.

I don't know if I understand ill-defined problems. When students struggle with them, I am not sure how to help them. I like it when there is structure and one correct answer. When there isn't structure and when there are multiple answers that make sense, I am not sure how to mark their work. We couldn't even demonstrate success with understanding the problem because there wasn't enough information in it to make sense of it.

Students didn't like these problems at all. Many referenced that the problems weren't really math problems and that it was too hard. Going through the four problem solving stages wasn't helpful. We couldn't craft a plan because we didn't know what to base it on.

There is a difference between each of the teachers' comments. The primary teacher refers to how much their students engaged in the ill-defined problems and how much students enjoyed the autonomy they had in working through the problem. The elementary and intermediate teachers did not have a similar experience with ill-defined problems. They both felt that traditional problem solving was not enough to solve the problem. Their students were not able to craft a plan because they could not find sufficient information in the problem. Elementary and intermediate teachers seem to be stuck on the fact that information is not front-loaded and that they are required to bring in relevant information themselves. This is not typical for the problems seen in many classrooms. Teachers have to appreciate the discrepancy and consider alternate ways to address ill-defined problems.

Summary

As demonstrated within this chapter, the four stages of problem solving outlined within the work of Polya (2004) are effective in solving defined problems. The four problem-solving stages provide students with the necessary steps to work through the three characteristics of defined problems (initial state, goal state, and obstacles). The first stage, understanding the problem, enables students to examine the problem and identify the information needed to solve the it. The second stage, crafting a plan, sees the student choosing a strategy based on the information provided and the goal state of the problem. The third stage, carrying out the plan, enables students the opportunity to execute the plan they selected. From this, students engage in the fourth stage, reviewing, where they can examine their work and check it against the problem.

These four stages of problem solving are effective when there is a clearly defined initial state, when obstacles are presented, and a goal state is identified. Things become problematic and an issue when the three characteristics are not present. Within ill-defined problems, students are not provided all the necessary information. Information is not front-loaded. Instead, the student must play an active and independent role in bringing information to the table. As such, when encountering ill-defined problems, it is not enough to rely on the work of Polya.

Ill-defined problems reflect what we encounter around us every day. We need to accept the fact that we rarely are given all the required information to solve problems. Many times, when we encounter problems in our everyday lives, we need to apply a mathematical lens to the situation and work from this perspective. When applying a mathematical lens to the problem, we are inserting our assumptions and understandings. This, in and of itself, is outside of the problem-solving stages outlined by Polya.

Moving forward, when presented with ill-defined problems, students need to engage in a framework that goes beyond traditional problem solving. Perhaps it is the fact that students rarely encounter ill-defined problems, or maybe it is the fact that we need students to move beyond following a process. What we need is for students to approach a problem from the perspective of thinking mathematically instead of doing mathematics. Through engaging with ill-defined problems, students will have the opportunity to become capable and confident math learners. It is about mathematizing student thinking so that students see the math in a situation and apply math to solve such situations. It is about moving beyond problem solving to engaging students in opportunities to mathematically model within everyday life contexts.

When we encounter problems in our everyday lives, we need to apply a mathematical lens to the situation and work from this perspective. When applying a mathematical lens to the problem, we are inserting our assumptions and understandings.

CHAPTER 3

Moving Toward Mathematical Modelling

By offering ill-defined problems students engage with mathematics that is reflective of their lived experiences. Mathematics should not, and does not, end at the school's doors.

For far too long there has been a disconnect between the mathematics students engage with in school and their everyday experiences outside of school. Mathematics has become compartmentalized. By offering ill-defined problems students engage with mathematics that is reflective of their lived experiences. Mathematics should not, and does not, end at the school's doors.

We must remove the barriers between school and lived experiences for our students' benefit. They need to find mathematics in their surroundings and use math to solve any problems they encounter. Students should mathematize their thinking and become capable and confident math learners. How do we do this? We use real-world situations in the classroom giving students opportunities to recognize math's significance. Using real-world situations will also strengthen the ability of students to infuse mathematics into their problem solving. Students will become more confident when mathematics can be applied to make sense of a problem and when it can be applied to solve a problem.

Modelling in Mathematics and Mathematical Modelling

Mathematizing student thinking necessitates students' ability to mathematically model. Now, we have heard the term *model* in mathematics for quite some time, however, it is important to pause and consider what it means to mathematically model. Consider the following responses teachers gave when they were asked to define what it means to mathematically model.

Modelling is important, especially for number sense. I will often have students model, or we call it represent, a number using 10-frames. This will allow students to go beyond the surface level and understand the quantity within the number. It also supports students in seeing a number in relation to the benchmark of 10. Another way we model is using a part-part-whole mat when decomposing numbers.

It is important to model in math. Before assigning any independent work, I make sure that I take time to model the concept and what is expected of my students when working with it. I usually will model the concept through a think aloud. By doing this, students have a clear understanding of what is expected of them. It is very much like a gradual release of responsibility.

Modelling is the foundation of math. Usually, I expect students to do most of the modelling work in elementary school. What I mean is that students will have represented whole numbers, decimals, and fractions before they come to my classroom. By the time I get students, we go right to the concept of using numbers. We may do a bit of work with algebra tiles, but mostly it is through symbols.

Each teacher references modelling as something that they are already familiar with and/or something that their students have done or do on a frequent basis. Within these three explanations, the elementary teacher explained modelling as a gradual release of responsibility, while the primary and intermediate teachers stressed modelling as another way of representing a concept, which focused on number for primary students and algebra for intermediate students.

To be clear, the modelling referenced in the comments are not what I am advocating for when stressing the need for mathematical modelling in solving ill-defined problems. So, although this may be the first time you have delved into the term modelling, let's take time to differentiate the phrases modelling in mathematics and mathematically modelling.

It shouldn't come as a surprise that the teachers referenced modelling the way they did. Consider it from the primary and intermediate teachers' perspectives. They each referenced modelling as a representation. In mathematics, a model has often been defined as a representation that demonstrates a mathematical concept. For example, let's look at some different models.

- Five-Frame
  - A visual that demonstrates the relation of a number to the number five
- Ten-Frame
  - A visual that demonstrates the relation of a number to the number 10

- Number Line
  - A visual that illustrates the order and magnitude of numbers
- Part-Part-Whole
  - A visual that illustrates how a number (whole) can be decomposed into two smaller numbers (parts)
- Base-Ten Blocks
  - Concrete objects that are used to represent the quantity of a number in relation to place value

The elementary teacher described modelling as being a gradual release of responsibility. This would be how modelling is described in many other subject areas that the teacher would be assigning.

However, both of these explanations of models, representations and a gradual release of responsibility, do not reflect what modelling means when referenced in mathematical modelling. In mathematical modelling, modelling is the verb. It is a process. Mathematical modelling is mathematizing a situation.

In mathematical modelling, modelling is the verb. It is a process. Mathematical modelling is mathematizing a situation.

A key distinction between **modelling in mathematics** and **mathematical modelling** is where students begin engaging in mathematics. Modelling in mathematics begins with mathematics (Van de Walle, Karp, Bay-Williams, & McGarvey, 2017). What I mean by this is that the task is embedded in math. Students are directed to model a concept (number, algebra, geometry, statistics) using a specific representation, whether it is concretely, pictorially, or symbolically. In contrast, mathematical modelling begins in the real-world, the everyday-life experiences of students (Pollak, 2007). Starting in the real-world and then moving into a mathematical situation is a significant distinction between mathematical modelling and modelling in mathematics. It is this reason that there is less familiarity with mathematical modelling as compared to modelling in mathematics. However, there is more to mathematical modelling than the differences I have introduced.

Defining Mathematical Modelling

Mathematical modelling is all about providing students with the ability to solve problems that are similar to their lived experiences. Mathematical modelling is about interrogating our experiences in the real-world and constructing models to situations we identify (Mason, 2001). It is about mathematizing thinking so that they can see the math that can be used to solve real-world problems.

Ill-defined problems are messy problems that are based on real-life situations. When engaged in mathematical modelling, students use mathematics to answer ill-defined problems. In applying mathematical modelling, creativity and critical thinking are necessities for students. Students make choices throughout the process from the time they engage with the problem to when they communicate their thinking. During mathematical modelling, students describe the real-world problem using mathematical language and concepts.

Let's be clear—mathematics is not the starting point in mathematical modelling. Instead, the student is presented with a problem that is based in the real world. In such a scenario, the real world is not just a context that is provided for a mathematical exercise. The reality within the problem is the starting point and the crux of the problem. Within this approach, both the real world and mathematics are taken with significance (Pollak, 2007).

Knowing the significance of both the real world and mathematics, it is important to emphasize that the real-world situation is the starting point in all things mathematical modelling. From this, the student then mathematizes the situation and their thinking of the situation to build a mathematical model that can place the real-world problem in mathematical terms. The student uses mathematics to explore the real-world problem and to understand it more clearly. It is about seeing math around us and using it to understand the situation. The student then returns to the problem within the context of the real-world situation.

Students must begin with the problem in the context of the real-world. By doing so the student mathematizes the situation and can remove the contextual element of the real-world. The focus should be on the mathematical language and concepts required to solve the problem. Once the work of mathematics is done, and the student feels confident that it can be used to solve the problem, they return the context of the situation to the real-world problem (Asempapa, 2015; Blum & Ferri, 2009).

What we have within mathematical modelling is a process that requires students to begin with the real-world problem that is contextualized. The student must remove the **contextualized** element and apply a mathematical framework allowing them to use mathematical language and concepts to frame and solve the problem. Once the student believes they have solved the mathematical problem, within a **decontextualized** state, they apply the solution to the context of the real-world problem to determine if their approach has solved the problem. Mathematical modelling is a method of translating the real-world situation—context—into a mathematical model—out of context. Then return to the real-world situation—context—to determine if the mathematization has addressed the issue presented in the initial problem (Asempapa, 2015; Blum & Ferri, 2009). The following visual depicts this process.

Mathematical modelling happens from the time students interpret the problem, make assumptions, decontextualize it to mathematize their thinking, apply their work to the contextualized real-world problem, and then interpret and communicate their understanding.

Within mathematical modelling, student investigations of real-world problems are important and significant. Students use mathematics as a way of making sense of the problem. Within the mathematical modelling process, students ask themselves math questions about real-world problems and use these questions to map out possible solution pathways. During the process, students are active learners, they generate pathways to find a solution. Instead of relying on information presented, they must consider the real-world problem, make assumptions about the parameters, and then use their **assumptions** to shape their work. As students engage in thinking, they often revise their approaches as they interpret results from their plan of action (Stohlmann & Albarracin, 2016; Wickstrom & Aytes, 2018). Mathematical modelling happens from the time students interpret the problem, make assumptions, decontextualize it to mathematize their thinking, apply their work to the contextualized real-world problem, and then interpret and communicate their understanding.

Mathematical modelling is counterproductive in comparison to traditional mathematics. Typically with traditional mathematics, students are presented with a defined problem. As we discovered in Chapter 1 defined problems are structured mathematical situations that may or may not be contextualized. When working with ill-defined problems, students are presented a real-world problem and must find ways to apply mathematics to reach a reasonable solution. As stated before, mathematical modelling requires students to apply a mathematical perspective to the work. In essence, students must mathematize their thinking.

Mathematical modelling, therefore, is an **iterative process** that has students go between the contextualized real-world problem and a decontextualized mathematical representation of the problem. This is not a "one and done" process. Students can go back and forth depending on the assumptions they make when managing the real problem to approach it from a realistic lens. After assumptions are made about the real-world problem, students will apply a mathematical perspective to their work to arrive at a solution. Then, they have to apply it to the contextualized real-world problem to see if it makes sense and is reasonable. This can happen multiple times before a solution is found.

Overall, there are four components involved within mathematical modelling. I am cognizant to use components instead of steps because when we think of steps, they tend to be linear—one and done. Students can engage with components multiple times to arrive at a solution. There are four components of mathematical modelling (Ministry of Education, 2020):

1. Understanding the problem
2. Analyzing the situation
3. Creating a mathematical model
4. Analyzing and assessing the model

The next visual represents the mathematical modelling process. There are three aspects within this diagram. The first aspect, are the numbers above or below the components. These numbers relate to the typical progression students take through the mathematical modelling process. The second aspect are the two-directional arrows. The arrows support the notion of mathematical modelling being an iterative process. When working through the components, it is not necessary to move from component four (analyzing and assessing the model) back to component three (creating a mathematical model). Instead, the student may move from component four to component one (understanding the problem) or component two (analyzing the situation). Depending on how students are clarifying, revising, or confirming their thinking, their next step will be influenced. The third aspect is not shaded among the four components. Component one (understanding the problem), component two (analyzing the situation) and component four (analyzing and assessing the model) are all shaded. This shading represents the components that are contextualized. When working within these components, the student is approaching thinking from the perspective of the context of the real-world problem. Component three (creating a mathematical model) is the student mathematizing the problem. It is during this component that the problem is decontextualized and the student works from a mathematical perspective.

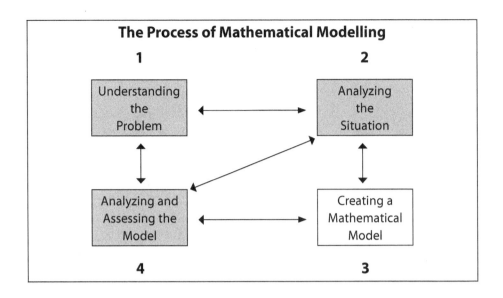

The Process of Mathematical Modelling

1. Understanding the Problem
2. Analyzing the Situation
3. Creating a Mathematical Model
4. Analyzing and Assessing the Model

Mathematical Modelling Process

The mathematical modelling process is one of iteration.

As previously stated, there are four components of mathematical modelling (Ministry of Education, 2020). Although the components are often discussed in isolation, it is important to note that the mathematical modelling process is one of iteration. Students will move through the various components and often return to them over time. In fact, it is not uncommon that as students mathematically model, they move between and across the components. Students will return to components once they change their thinking and/or experience a stumbling block that may contradict their previous work. It is during this iteration that students refine their thinking and extend the mathematical model to a contextualized setting.

Before I move any further, I want to pause and stress how the mathematical modelling process is often structured as a collaborative endeavor. There is much to gain, in terms of mathematical understanding, when students have an opportunity to discuss ideas, compare and contrast approaches, question their thoughts and the thoughts of others, and work through stumbling blocks. When engaged in problems outside of school, it is natural that people work together to make sense of the problem and work toward a solution. The same can be said for mathematical experiences in the classroom. Therefore, when considering the mathematical modelling process and the four components, please do not think that students must work on their own. Collaboration and communication are significant parts of the process that support students in making sense of the situation and math, as well as working toward a reasonable solution.

Each of the four components are discussed next. Each component is described and questions are used to guide students as they work within each component.

Understanding the Problem

Students take the time to understand the ill-defined problem that relates to the real world. This understanding is much more than surface level. Students must recognize the context of the problem, what is being asked, and what information is required for solving the problem.

Questions that students can ask themselves or others when working within this component are:

- What do I know?
- What can I bring to this problem?
- What do I need to know?

Analyzing the Situation

Students take the time to refine the real-world problem to make it work. Students will make assumptions to refine the parameters of the problem. They will idealize the situation by identifying conditions. These assumptions and conditions provide structure to the messy, ill-defined problem.

Questions that students can ask themselves or others when working within this component are:

- What assumptions can I make regarding this situation?
- How can I make this situation workable? What changes? What stays the same?

Creating a Mathematical Model

Students will decontextualize the problem through mathematics. Students will take time to consider the structured problem, based on their work from the previous component. By making assumptions and identifying conditions, students can now approach the problem from a mathematical perspective. Students will decide on the mathematical language and concepts to apply, and the method of applying such mathematics.

Questions that students can ask themselves or others when working within this component are:

- What mathematical language applies to this problem?
- What mathematical concept applies to this problem?
- What representations and support can be applied to build a mathematical model?

Analyzing and Assessing the Model

Students will apply their mathematical model to the context of the real-world problem. This is when students reintroduce their work to the context of the problem. They question the validity of their model as it refers to the real-world problem, the assumptions made and the conditions they identified. Students will determine if their mathematical model provides a reasonable solution to the real-world problem and whether alternative models exist.

Questions that students can ask themselves or others when working within this component are:

- Does my mathematical model lead to a reasonable solution to the problem?
- Do other alternative mathematical models exist?

Instructional Goals

Mathematical modelling is a process where students engage with real-world problems that requires them to move between the contextualized problem, decontextualized mathematics, and then back to the contextualized problem. Mathematical modelling requires students to mathematize their thinking so that they can effectively determine a pathway to a reasonable solution. However, when considering mathematical modelling from the perspective of instructional goals, teachers have two choices: mathematical modelling as vehicle and mathematical modelling as content (Galbraith 2012).

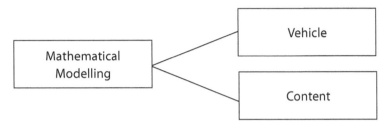

Mathematical modelling as content shifts the focus to supporting students in developing their proficiency in applying the four components of mathematical modelling.

When selecting mathematical modelling as vehicle for the instructional goal, teachers have decided to use mathematical modelling to support student mathematical understanding. Within this approach, teachers employ mathematical modelling to structure student experiences during mathematics. The rationale of doing such is that mathematical modelling provides students with opportunities to explore new math concepts or practice concepts in real-world contexts. When selecting mathematical modelling as vehicle, teachers are less concerned with students having proficiency in modelling and more concerned with students having opportunities to develop their understanding of mathematical concepts.

The alternative to selecting mathematical modelling as vehicle for the instructional goal is to select mathematical modelling as content. Mathematical modelling as content shifts the focus to supporting students in developing their proficiency in applying the four components of mathematical modelling. It is about students effectively applying the mathematical modelling process to solve real-world problems. The goal is for students to not only understand how to mathematically model but also to be able to apply it effectively when working through ill-defined problems.

These two instructional goals of mathematical modelling—vehicle and content—are not mutually exclusive. The teacher can choose to weave throughout both goals, so long as the integrity of each is upheld. What needs to be considered, though, is that when sharing the instructional goal with students, that they honor that goal so that students can recognize where they are at in relation to the particular instructional goal.

Higher Order Thinking

Higher order thinking skills are used by students engaged in mathematical modelling. When applying mathematical modelling to solve ill-defined problems, students employ the following higher order thinking: creativity and innovation, critical thinking and problem solving, communication, collaboration, and contribution to knowledge production. At different points of the mathematical modelling process, students engage in mathematizing real-world problems.

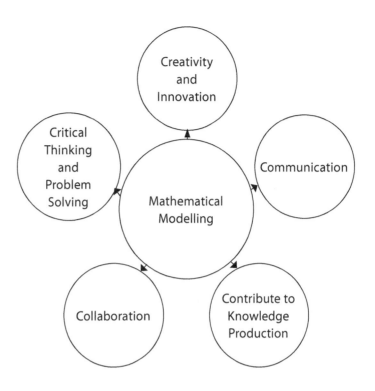

When engaged in mathematical modelling, students demonstrate creativity and innovation. Whether it is how they frame the problem into a mathematical situation or how they determine and select a strategy to solve the problem, students must employ a level of creativity and innovation. There is no set of rules or questions to ask that will ensure a solution when mathematically modelling. Students must, independent of the teacher, recognize the parameters and set out on a path that they believe will lead them to a solution that makes sense in relation to the original real-world problem. Throughout the process of mathematical modelling, students will have to make decisions that are nonformulaic and non-routine. They must step outside the box and consider what may work and then apply that to the model they have developed.

Critical thinking is embedded through each of the four components of mathematical modelling. Students have to pause and consider each aspect from the moment they are presented with the real-world problem. They must make sense of it, make assumptions, and develop the model to apply to the decontextualized problem. They must work through stumbling blocks since the process is non-routine. Students must approach each decision point from a critical perspective as mathematical modelling is an iterative process that requires students to reflect on their decisions and determine if they are working toward a solution that makes sense.

Communication is crucial to working through the iterative process of mathematical modelling and in sharing your thinking with others. Whether you are working with a group or individually, it is necessary to be able to effectively communicate your understanding so that your work is transparent and others can determine if the process you applied is accurate. Communication provides others with insight into the many decisions you used to reach the solution so that they can determine if your work is replicable in other situations. Such communication can be oral and/or written.

Critical thinking is embedded through each of the four components of mathematical modelling. Students have to pause and consider each aspect from the moment they are presented with the real-world problem.

Collaboration plays a role in many mathematical modelling experiences. When mathematically modelling, students may be assigned groups. When in groups, it is imperative that students have the skills and abilities to work as a team to reach a solution. Collaboration does not mean that each student has an assigned role to complete independently of others. Instead, collaboration is the ability to work in a team setting and contribute to the overall growth and success of the team. Collaboration involves the ability to demonstrate accountability to teammates and the ability to take initiative and self-direction. The ability to be flexible depends on what happens during the team's engagement with the problem.

Contribution to **knowledge production** is an important aspect of mathematical modelling. As mathematical modelling involves students working through ill-defined problems, there is not a set pathway or predetermined solution. Instead, students must be able to approach the problem from a stance that their prior knowledge and experiences will be significant in choosing a pathway that results in a meaningful solution. As such, students will actively construct new understandings that will not only benefit themselves as math learners but also support the learning of others when they can share their work. The key to mathematical modelling is the generation of knowledge and understanding, of which will support students in developing their higher ordering thinking skills.

When students engage in mathematical modelling, their purpose may be to arrive at a reasonable solution, but they are indirectly strengthening thinking skills. The higher order thinking skills that students foster when mathematically modelling will not only support students in developing their mathematical understanding but will contribute to creating capable and confident math learners.

The higher order thinking skills that students foster when mathematically modelling will not only support students in developing their mathematical understanding but will contribute to creating capable and confident math learners.

The Need for Social-Emotional Learning Skills

Within mathematical modelling, students take the position of being active in their learning. Students are generators of knowledge and information when working through ill-defined problems as opposed to being recipients of knowledge and information when working through defined problems. Being generators of knowledge and information as they work through ill-defined problems provides students with opportunities to develop their social-emotional learning skills.

Let's consider six **social-emotional learning skills**: (1) identification and management of emotions, (2) stress management and coping, (3) positive motivation and perseverance, (4) healthy relationships, (5) self-awareness and a sense of identity, and (6) critical and creative thinking (Ministry of Education, 2020). While these six social-emotional learning skills are not explicitly stated as academic performance indicators, they are inherent to the academic success of students. The proceeding table outlines the six social-emotional learning skills, a brief explanation of each skill, and the strategies embedded within each skill related to mathematics.

Social-Emotional Learning Skill	Brief Description	Embedded Strategies in Relation to Mathematics
Identification and management of emotions	The ability to identify and manage emotions and emotional responses when engaged in learning.	• Recognize the range of emotions they may encounter. • Understand the connections between thoughts, feelings, and actions. • Manage emotions when problem solving and apply self-regulation.
Stress management and coping	The recognition that stress will arise when engaged in problem solving and that they can apply coping strategies to build resilience.	• Work through stumbling blocks. • Understand coping strategies build resilience.
Positive motivation and perseverance	A positive disposition is important as they work through a problem. Recognize that mistakes are opportunities for learning and supports students' perseverance.	• Practice perseverance. • Embrace mistakes as a necessary part of learning. • Try different methods when problem solving.
Healthy relationships	The ability to work cooperatively and collaboratively with others strengthens the work and leads to finding solutions.	• Be cooperative and collaborative with others. • Consider the perspectives of others.
Self-awareness and a sense of identity	Know oneself as a learner will assist students as they work through a problem. An accurate awareness of their own understanding supports students as they frame and support their abilities to problem solve effectively.	• Know oneself. • Communicate thinking about mathematics. • Build identity as a math learner. • Monitor progress in skill development.

Critical and creative thinking	The ability to critically examine a problem and the decisions they have made while working through the problem enables students to have an overall picture of where they are at in the problem-solving process. The ability to creatively determine a problem-solving approach leads students to think outside the box and increase their chances of determining the solution.	• Make connections between mathematical concepts. • Evaluate the thinking in the problem-solving process. • Assess possible strategies. • Think outside the box when a traditional approach is not effective.

Social-emotional learning skills contribute to students developing confidence in their ability to work through productive struggle.

As seen in the table above, when students can develop their social-emotional learning skills, they will see an improvement in their academic performance. Social-emotional learning skills support students in understanding mathematical language and concepts as well as being able to apply the skills when working through problems. As a result of supporting students in strengthening their mathematical understanding, social-emotional learning skills contribute to students developing confidence in their ability to work through productive struggle. Students develop into capable and confident math learners.

Cultural Relevance

By assigning an ill-defined problem based in real-world context, students are afforded opportunities to connect mathematics and their lived experiences. As such, students are immersed in problems that are personal and meaningful. Through addressing the segregation of student lived experiences and the mathematics they encounter in school, mathematical modelling is a way in which mathematical instruction and understanding is brought closer for all students (Pollak, 2003).

When working through the mathematical modelling process, students have multiple opportunities to draw on their funds of knowledge (Anhalt, Staats, & Civil, 2018). The problem presented can be a significant form of motivation. When students see relevancy in the problem, their ability to make connections increases, as compared to traditional math problems. It is because of this that students are provided multiple opportunities to apply cultural awareness to their problem-solving.

During the initial components of mathematical modelling, students use their cultural understanding to craft assumptions that allow them to refine the ill-defined problem. The cultural awareness students bring to the process is used as the reference point as to whether the assumption is accurate or not. From this refining, students then mathematize the situation. Then, in the mathematical modelling process, students will apply the mathematized work to the original problem to see if the solution makes sense and if it addresses the original problem. When judging the reasonableness of the work, students must rely on their cultural awareness so that they can determine if the work is in alignment with the parameters presented within the problem. Mathematical modelling is an iterative process in which students use their lived experiences and cultural awareness to engage in meaningful problem solving.

The Teacher's Role

Teachers play a crucial role in the mathematical modelling experiences of their students. While students are independent learners and generators of knowledge, teachers work to craft an environment and experience that will support students in mathematizing their thinking as they become capable and confident math learners.

Consider the following comments teachers made when asked to explain their role as the teacher when students are engaged in mathematical modelling.

PRIMARY EXAMPLE: A TEACHER EXPLAINS

Mathematical modelling can be tricky in Grade 1 through Grade 3. I don't know how to support my students in starting the work without being prescriptive. If I am prescriptive, doesn't that negate the whole purpose of mathematical modelling?

ELEMENTARY EXAMPLE: A TEACHER EXPLAINS

Finding the right question is an important part of math modelling. The problem is finding such questions. My math program doesn't really do much with mathematical modelling and I don't feel that I can craft such questions. So, without having the questions I really haven't been doing much mathematical modelling in the classroom.

INTERMEDIATE EXAMPLE: A TEACHER EXPLAINS

I appreciate that mathematical modelling will provide my students with opportunities to see the relevance in math and how math can be used in their lives outside of school. However, I struggle with knowing how to best bring mathematical modelling into the classroom. Students are supposed to be independent and creative when working through the problem, but how do I support this when I'm not sure where they are coming from or whether their approach to solving the problem is a great way to do it?

It is fair to say that while teachers appreciate the complexity involved in mathematical modelling, there is ambiguity in how they go about defining the necessary characteristics of teachers in facilitating mathematical modelling. To combat this ambiguity, the following table lists the characteristics and skills teachers require when engaging students in mathematical modelling. For each characteristic and/or skill, I provide a brief explanation.

Characteristics and Skills	Brief Description
Facilitation Skills	The ability to facilitate discussion as opposed to managing the learning. It is imperative that students take the leadership role when mathematical modelling. The teacher uses facilitation skills to support their role as a guide so that students follow a solution path that they have developed. The teacher makes suggestions and asks questions when necessary.
Questioning	Asking the right type of questions can create a mathematical modelling experience that promotes student engagement and autonomy. Questions need to be reflective of students' lived experiences whereby students begin with the context and then apply math. When questions are crafted with suitable contexts, students have an entry point to begin their work to solve the problem.
Problem-Solving Knowledge	Having an understanding of problem solving will provide the teacher with confidence that productive struggle is inherent in mathematical modelling. Students will face cognitive demand when working through the mathematical modelling process and teachers need to be aware of this so that they do not intervene and do the work for students.
Content Knowledge	When engaged with mathematical modelling, students will have the opportunity to apply a variety of mathematical concepts. The teacher needs to be cognizant of this and recognize whether the mathematical content students have selected will support them in finding a solution. In addition, the teacher must understand whether students are accurately applying the mathematical content they have selected as part of their model.

Access to a Variety of Representations and Tools	It is important that the teacher has access to a variety of representations and tools when students are engaged in mathematical modelling. Having such a variety will enable the teacher to offer students multiple choices in their modelling and will allow students the opportunity to select the best option for their work. Access to manipulatives, software programs, internet sites, calculators, and visuals are valuable supports teachers can make available to students.
Patience	Patience may seem like common sense, but it cannot be understated. Mathematical modelling takes time, much more time than solving traditional, defined problems. Teachers need to recognize this and demonstrate patience in letting the students work through the various components of the mathematical modelling process. Being impatient can result in students not having the freedom to work through a problem and may hinder their level of autonomy and engagement.
Understand the Mathematical Modelling Process	Having an understanding of the mathematical modelling process supports the teacher in facilitating the process as opposed to directing it. Understanding the mathematical modelling process ensures that the teacher recognizes how students will move through the components in an iterative manner. The teacher will appreciate the many decision points students make when mathematically modelling, from the initial point of entry to sharing their thinking.

Effective teaching of mathematical modelling requires teachers to have multiple knowledge bases such as understanding their students and their experiences; understanding content knowledge; understanding pedagogical knowledge; and being able to engage students in experiences that will promote independence in learning. Overall, engaging students in mathematical modelling requires teachers to facilitate student learning in ways that are more open and less predictable when compared to the traditional approach to mathematics (Blum & Ferri, 2009).

The Student's Role

When working through the mathematical modelling process, students encounter numerous obstacles. It is necessary to be creative and critical thinkers if they want to be successful in determining a reasonable solution. Students need to step outside the realm of doing math and become comfortable in mathematizing their thinking. As such, students take the lead in applying mathematics to solve a problem and being able to communicate their thinking to others.

The following student comments explain how they feel about mathematical modelling and the skills required to be successful when mathematically modelling.

PRIMARY EXAMPLE: A STUDENT EXPLAINS

It can be hard. Sometimes, I don't know what exactly to do to solve the problem. It can take a lot of work.

ELEMENTARY EXAMPLE: A STUDENT EXPLAINS

Mathematical modelling is about solving everyday life problems. The problems we have to solve aren't like the regular math problems. There is a lot more thinking that you have to do and you have to know the math really well.

INTERMEDIATE EXAMPLE: A STUDENT EXPLAINS

When you are given a question to answer that requires mathematical modelling, it is more than just following a series of steps. You have to think about the problem, think about what you need to consider to solve it, and then choose an approach that makes the most sense. After all this, you have to see if your work makes sense. It's about working through challenging situations.

> The students must take an active stance in their learning and rely on their understanding, of both the real-world context and mathematics.

It is fair to say that in each of the students' comments they directly reference the level of thinking required to work through the mathematical modelling process. It is not about following predetermined steps. Instead, the students must take an active stance in their learning and rely on their understanding, of both the real-world context and mathematics, to arrive at a solution that makes sense and that they can explain. Engagement is crucial if students are to dedicate themselves to the problem and want to work through the obstacles to reach a solution that makes sense. Students must be independent so that they do not rely on their teacher to make sense of the real-world problem or to select the mathematics that will help them work through the problem. Depth of knowledge is a necessity. Not only must students have the ability to recognize and make meaning of the context provided in the problem, they should be able to have a repertoire of mathematical concepts to apply to mathematize the situation. Having confidence in both their understanding of mathematics and their ability to problem solve will aid the students in being able to mathematically model. To highlight these four characteristics and skills (engagement, independence, depth of knowledge and confidence), I have crafted the following table to explain each.

Characteristics and Skills	Brief Description
Engagement	Student engagement can be a determining factor in students having success solving a problem. When engaged in the problem, students take more ownership and are more likely to be motivated in reaching a solution. The problem is relevant to them. By providing students with a real-world problem, their engagement increases because they can make a connection to the situation. By making a connection, their interest and curiosity in solving the problem may be piqued.
Independence	An independent learner is a student who is more persistent in solving problems. When problem solving, the independent learner demonstrates self-regulation as they work through highs and lows. Independent learners view themselves as developing math expertise and they have the confidence to make mathematical decisions to work through the problem. They have a repertoire of tools available to them and can decide which tool to apply as they work through the problem.
Depth of Knowledge	Having a depth of knowledge means that students can apply current understanding to the mathematical modelling experience. From the perspective of their lived experiences, students can make connections to the real-world context of the problem and use these connections to help them make sense of the problem and identify critical aspects that are present or that must be added to make sense of the problem. From the perspective of mathematics, the ability to understand mathematical concepts and processes will aid students in recognizing how to apply mathematics to the problem so that they can mathematize the situation.

Confidence	Confidence plays an important role in how likely students are to work through the mathematical modelling process to completion. If students are confident in their thinking, it is probable that they work through stumbling blocks. Confidence provides the motivation for students to persevere. Confidence also contributes to students believing that they are capable math learners and that they do have the ability to reach a solution.

Mathematical modelling requires students to have characteristics and skills that will not only support them in mathematizing the situation but also in working through the stumbling blocks they will encounter.

Mathematical modelling requires students to have characteristics and skills that will not only support them in mathematizing the situation but also in working through the stumbling blocks they will encounter. Whether it is their engagement with the problem, their ability to independently navigate the mathematical modelling process, their understanding of the world and mathematics, or their confidence in themselves as mathematicians, students will need to recognize that they cannot rely on others to solve the problem. They need to be generators of knowledge and understanding. For students to be successful in mathematical modelling, they need to be capable and confident math learners who can mathematize their thinking.

Summary

Throughout the chapter we have seen how mathematical modelling is a process that has many decision points. After being presented with an ill-defined problem, students must craft assumptions that will help them establish parameters so that they can work with the problem. From these assumptions, students then mathematize the situation by applying a mathematical model. Students rely on mathematics to reach a solution that makes sense and that can be applied to the original ill-defined problem. Students, then, communicate their work to others.

In the components of mathematical modelling, students must move between a contextualized and decontextualized setting. Starting with context, the student needs to decontextualize the situation so that they can apply a mathematical concept to reach a plausible solution. Students, though, have to return to the contextualized setting to determine if the mathematics accurately addresses the original problem posed to students. A key support to students when working in the contextualized setting is their cultural awareness. Students rely on their ability to make sense of the context based on their lived experiences. This cultural relevancy promotes engagement, independence, and confidence.

Although each of the components of mathematical modelling are presented within this chapter, the overview is brief. We will examine each of the components in subsequent chapters and understand what is required in every component.

4

Understanding Ill-Defined Problems

Mathematical modelling is an iterative process that requires students to work through a real-world problem. Within this iterative process, students must recognize when they should change their approach from either a contextual or a decontextualized perspective. As we have seen in earlier discussions students must be critical thinkers, creative, persistent, and flexible when working through various thinking points within a mathematical modelling experience.

The diagram on the next page represents mathematical modelling. The diagram identifies and numbers the four components. The numbers do not indicate steps, but rather emphasize the key categories captured within the mathematical modelling process. Each of the four components—understanding the problem, analyzing the situation, creating a mathematical model, and analyzing and assessing the model—are comprised of many smaller aspects.

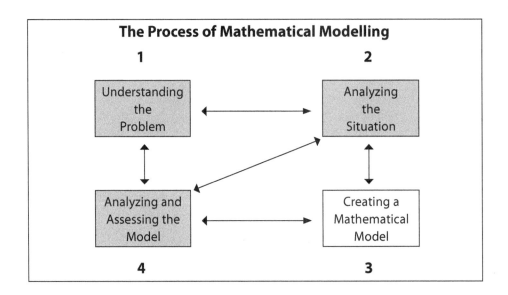

The Process of Mathematical Modelling

1   2

Understanding the Problem ⟷ Analyzing the Situation

Analyzing and Assessing the Model ⟷ Creating a Mathematical Model

4   3

This chapter, along with the next three chapters, will address each of the four mathematical modelling components. I will identify the component, detail the roles of teachers and students, and share student work samples, to demonstrate student thinking within the component. The chapter will end with an opportunity for the reader to engage in understanding the problem component of mathematical modelling.

What's Involved in Understanding the Problem

In the component, understanding the problem, students explore and examine real-world questions and the context in which they are presented. During this exploration, students recognize what is being asked and what information is necessary in solving the problem.

As part of this component, students can ask themselves, or others—if working in collaboration—the following questions:

- What do I know?
- What can I bring to this problem?
- What do I need to know?

First, in understanding the given problem the student must comprehend the situational model. The situational model is the real-world problem assigned to students. When reading the problem students must identify what is being asked. This is not always clear. Consider the problems we encounter outside of school, very rarely are they presented the same way that defined problems are—context provided with a question posed at the end. In real-world problems, or ill-defined problems, the students may have to read the problem and infer what is being asked. Once students make this determination, they should pause and consider what information is necessary to solve the problem. Students must also determine which information is superfluous. This can be a challenging process for students if it does not reflect any experience that they may have encountered in mathematics.

Students are the decision-makers; students pose questions to better grasp the problem and what is being asked. As such, students take responsibility for how they will understand and investigate the problem.

The challenge in understanding the problem is the additional complexity placed on students. Instead of reading a question within the problem, students must infer its meaning. They must consider what is written, analyze the context within the problem, and then contribute their own ideas. This approach requires students to take an independent learning approach to problem solving. In this perspective, students are the decision-makers; students pose questions to better grasp the problem and what is being asked. As such, students take responsibility for how they will understand and investigate the problem.

Demonstrating understanding of the problem is much more than being able to restate it. Simply restating does not imply students understand the problem. Instead, students should restate the problem in their own words, highlight important information, remove superfluous information, identify the question that is being asked, and provide an account of the context within which the problem is presented.

The Teacher's Role

Although mathematical modelling is a process in which students take the lead in their learning, the teacher does play an important part. The role of the teacher is not to be a manager or supplier of knowledge; instead, the teacher is the facilitator. The teacher must possess specific skills in supporting the student as they work through the mathematical modelling process.

Consider the following teachers' comments about their roles during mathematical modelling. The comments refer to the first component—understanding the problem—of mathematical modelling.

PRIMARY EXAMPLE: A TEACHER EXPLAINS

I thought it would be the easiest part of mathematical modelling. I was wrong. It was definitely challenging for students to understand the problem. I had to help students by asking questions. I just couldn't sit back and do nothing.

ELEMENTARY EXAMPLE: A TEACHER EXPLAINS

I have been working more and more with real-world problems and math modelling. While students are getting a bit more comfortable with the process, they still struggle with understanding the problem. They look to me to give them hints about what the question is. I have been working on my wait time and not answering questions that they could answer themselves. It takes patience.

INTERMEDIATE EXAMPLE: A TEACHER EXPLAINS

I've found that I need to work on my facilitation skills if I want students to develop as math modelers and strengthen their ability to understand the problem. I need to get better at re-framing my students' questions and finding ways to support understanding instead of answering their questions.

Each of the teachers realize that they must facilitate the learning experience of their students. It is not about giving hints or providing answers. It is about using facilitation skills such as questioning, reframing language, and patience. The students should be able to understand the problem, and the only way this will happen is if the teacher supports their students in working through stumbling blocks instead of doing the work for them.

When using questioning to support student learning, it is important to consider what students are currently thinking (Polya, 2004). Teachers can consider the students' understanding of the problem, their ability to make connections with the problem, and whether they are encountering issues that may relate to social-emotional learning. When teachers consider what students may be thinking, they can craft questions that will assist students to move forward.

Teachers may be tempted to answer their students' questions. While this may seem to be a productive way to move student thinking forward, it may cause more stumbling blocks for the students. Students may rely more on the teacher to answer their questions. This is not the outcome we are hoping to achieve. Students work through their own stumbling blocks and use questioning as a form of metacognition. Relying on their teachers contradicts independent learning, which is a cornerstone of mathematical modelling.

When students ask questions to seek help teachers can redirect the conversation to support students' independence and perseverance. For instance, should students ask what the problem is about or what information in the problem is necessary, teachers have two approaches to take. First, teachers can stay silent and provide wait time for students. This requires students to work through their questions themselves. Second, teachers could ask students to explain what they know about the problem. Having students recount what they know is a metacognitive task where the students consolidate their understanding and can use this to move forward. Providing students wait time after they ask questions will provide additional opportunities for productive struggle and perseverance.

When teachers are asked questions by students trying to figure out the problem, they can ask any of the following questions to guide student thinking forward (Butler Wolf, 2015):

- Have you read the whole situation?
- What is the problem about?
- What are you supposed to find out?
- Can you tell me what the problem is about in your own words?
- Can you draw a picture of the problem?
- Can you represent the problem using concrete objects?
- Have you seen another problem like this one?
- Does this problem remind you of anything you have experienced?

Another benefit of teacher questioning is that it acts as a support for students to move from nonproductive struggle to productive struggle.

The questioning approach allows for the student to better understand the problem. This **strategic questioning** approach will guide students through stumbling blocks, while at the same time, support students in persevering. Another benefit of teacher questioning is that it acts as a support for students to move from nonproductive struggle to productive struggle. **Nonproductive struggle** will lead students to give up. Effective questioning can be applied so that students recognize their emotional state and use this recognition to move forward in understanding the problem.

In addition to supporting perseverance, effective questioning can be applied by the teacher to strengthen the classroom discourse. Through questioning, teachers can identify key mathematical vocabulary, highlight specific aspects of the problem, and assist students in communicating their mathematical understanding in an accurate manner. Using questioning as a facilitation skill can be effective in not only guiding students through the problem they are currently working on, but also assist them in building tools that can be applied to problems they encounter in the future.

A key aspect to using questioning to facilitate student learning and understanding of the problem is that the teacher anticipates possible students' misconceptions. Teachers can create questions that are relatable and provide a purpose to students. Such questions can assist students to move forward toward understanding the problem.

The Student's Role

Throughout the book I have stated how the mathematical modelling framework gives students the ability to make many decisions within the process. Within the component—understanding the problem—students must apply creativity, flexibility, and critical thinking in making these decisions. By definition autonomy in learning promotes student independence from the teacher to make meaning and decide on next steps.

Consider the following comments students provided to describe their approach in understanding the problem.

PRIMARY EXAMPLE: A STUDENT EXPLAINS

My class uses the three-read strategy to solve word problems. But it doesn't work when I have to solve problems based on real-life. It doesn't matter how many times I read it, I don't know what the problem is asking.

ELEMENTARY EXAMPLE: A STUDENT EXPLAINS

Understanding the problem is hard. It is not like normal word problems. When we read the problems, the question isn't always there. We have to read through it and decide on what the problem is and what question needs to be answered.

INTERMEDIATE EXAMPLE: A STUDENT EXPLAINS

When the teacher assigns mathematical modelling, I know that I will have to do more thinking. It requires me to figure out what is happening in the problem and then I think about what is necessary and what's not. It sounds easy here, but it takes a lot of time. And, how I understand the problem may not be the exact same way as another person understands the problem. What a person brings to the problem will shape how they approach the rest of their work.

It is apparent that regardless of the grade level, students find understanding the problem to be challenging. It is not about following a predetermined sequence of steps. Instead, the student must approach the real-world problem from a perspective of meaning-making. The student must consider the problem as a whole, identify necessary and unnecessary information, and then, based on the context of the problem, determine what is being asked. As the intermediate student explains, this approach to understanding the problem can lead to work that is nonformulaic. Depending on the perspective of students, the understanding of the problem component may be unique from one student or group to the next.

The opinions students have provided shows that understanding the problem can be a difficult task. Students need to have the confidence that they can make sense of the problem, understand what is being asked, and work through the challenge. While it may be difficult at first with practice students will become more confident.

With confidence comes independence. If students have confidence in their mathematical skills—the content and the process of modelling—students will be able to work through the first component. Independence means students are active learners who do not rely on their teacher to help them move forward. They are setting themselves up for success by becoming more independent. Also, independence is a crucial aspect required because not all the information is presented within the problem. Instead, students must generate information that will assist them in understanding the context and helping them frame their next decision.

> When understanding the problem, students must not only identify necessary information, but also generate questions that will assist them in making meaning of the real-world problem.

When understanding the problem, students must not only identify necessary information, but also generate questions that will assist them in making meaning of the real-world problem. Having a real-world problem presented within a contextual setting requires students to pose questions so that they can generate an understanding of what is presented in the problem and help identify information that may not have been given. It is for this reason Wickstrom and Aytes (2018) stressed that **problem posing** is equally as important as problem solving.

Embedded within and supportive of confidence, independence, and questioning, is critical thinking. Students who can analyze real-world problems are able to examine them as a way of understanding the situation. Critical thinking enables the student to take a closer look at the problem and consider it from different perspectives. Mastering these critical thinking techniques helps students make sense of problems and move forward in the mathematical modelling process.

Student Work Samples

Let's explore the component, understanding the problem, in action. We will review the work samples from a primary, elementary, and intermediate student. For each work sample, I will share the real-world problem, highlight aspects of student thinking and the facilitation questions that teachers asked the students as they were engaged with the task.

Primary

The following problem was assigned to primary students.

> *The Kindergarten classroom recognized that many of their supplies for centers were needing to be replaced. The teacher shared that they needed to buy new supplies but that they had a limited budget.*

The table highlights the primary student's thinking as they engaged with the problem.

STUDENT THINKING

What do I know?

- I know that the problem is about buying supplies for a Kindergarten classroom.
- The supplies that the Kindergarten class had need replacing.
- There is a limited budget to buy the supplies.

What question(s) need to be answered?

- What supplies are going to be bought?

What information is needed?

- What is the budget?
- What supplies will be bought?
- How much are the supplies?

What experience can I bring to the problem?

- I know the kind of things that I would like to play with in Kindergarten.
- I know some of the prices of these things. I know where to find the exact prices.

The following table highlights the questions the teacher asked as they were facilitating this component of mathematical modelling.

TEACHER FACILITATION QUESTIONS

- What is the problem about?
- What are you supposed to find out?
- Does this problem remind you of anything you have experienced?

Elementary

The following problem was assigned to elementary students.

> The local elementary school was selected as the site for the cross-county meet. As part of holding this meet, the school had to decide how to accommodate people wanting to watch the meet.

The table highlights the elementary student's thinking as they engaged with the problem.

What do I know?

- The school was holding a cross-country meet.
- The school needs to figure how to have people watch the meet.

What question(s) need to be answered?

- What is the plan to place people that watch the meet?

What information is needed?

- How many people will want to watch?
- What is the size of the area that can hold people?
- How many people can fit into the area?
- How many people usually run at these cross-country meets?

What experience can I bring to the problem?

- I've been to a game before and usually each athlete can only have 3–4 people come and watch.
- When sports happen outside, more people can come because there is more space to put them.

The following table highlights the questions the elementary teacher asked as they were facilitating this component of mathematical modelling.

- What is the problem about?
- What are you supposed to find out?
- Can you rephrase the problem in your own words?
- Does any of this problem seem familiar to you? Can you make any connections to it?

Intermediate

The following problem was assigned to intermediate students.

> In planning end-of-year activities, the school administration decide that the Grade 8 students would go on a field trip. The administration wanted to know what the cost per student would be for such a trip.

The table highlights the intermediate student's thinking as they engaged with the problem.

What do I know?

- Grade 8 students are going on a field trip.
- The school needs to figure out the cost per student.

What question(s) need to be answered?

- What is the cost per student?

What information is needed?

- Where is the field trip?
- What are the factors included in the cost (travel, accommodations, food, and chaperones)?
- Are students paying for any of the field trip?

What experience can I bring to the problem?

- When I have been on field trips before, I usually pay for my own food.
- Chaperones usually pay for their own food.
- Most field trips are usually 1-day so a hotel isn't needed.
- Students usually pay a small amount for part of the trip.

The following table highlights the questions the intermediate teacher asked as they were facilitating this component of mathematical modelling.

TEACHER FACILITATION QUESTIONS

- What is the problem about?
- What are you supposed to find out?
- Can you rephrase the problem in your own words?
- What experiences can you bring to understanding the problem?

Anticipating Classroom Connections

We have just reviewed an example of a real-world problem, the student thinking process to understand the problem, and questions from the teacher to facilitate student learning. Let's now examine a few other real-world problems aimed at each grade level. In each problem, consider the following:

- Anticipate how students will answer the four questions:
  - What do I know?
  - What question(s) need to be answered?
  - What information is needed?
  - What experience can I bring to the problem?
- Consider facilitation questions you can have in your repertoire to support student understanding of the real-world problem.

Primary Real-World Problem

Consider the following real-world problem assigned to primary students:

You are planning to have a birthday party and would like to give everyone a gift bag as they leave. How much will this cost?

Elementary Real-World Problem

Consider the following real-world problem assigned to elementary students:

As a way to store items that students play with while on the playground, the leadership group decided to build storage bins. The principal agreed to this so long as the cost of the project was effectively managed.

Intermediate Real-World Problem

Consider the following real-world problem assigned to intermediate students:

The population of your community is growing. There are already limited housing options available to current residents. What can the community do?

Summary

As can be seen within this chapter, understanding the problem is the cornerstone of the mathematical modelling work for students. Without understanding the problem, how are students expected to frame it, apply a mathematical model, or reach a solution? Better still, how can students be expected to apply this model in the context of the original problem to see if the mathematization of the situation makes sense and is applicable?

For students to have success with understanding the problem, they must be able to have creativity, flexibility, and critical thinking. These aspects will support students as they work through a real-world problem that is ill-defined and that requires students to take an active stance in framing the problem to be solved.

Students will encounter stumbling blocks as they work toward understanding the problem. Overcoming such stumbling blocks will require students to have confidence and independence so they do not rely on others to make progress and can question both the problem and its context so that they can make meaning. These skills that are required not only represent aspects of mathematical processes but also social-emotional learning skills. It is imperative that students recognize their emotions and know their emotions can play a part in the mathematical modelling process.

Teachers play a key role in supporting students as they work toward understanding the problem. Although teachers should not manage or direct student thinking, they do need to facilitate the experience. This facilitation takes the form of strategic questioning. Teachers need to be able to use questioning techniques to move student learning forward.

With the goal of building capable and confident math leaners, students must accept and realize they need to contribute to knowledge production if they want to be able to understand the problem they are working through.

> Overcoming such stumbling blocks will require students to have confidence and independence so they do not rely on others to make progress and can question both the problem and its context so that they can make meaning.

CHAPTER 5

Analyzing the Situation

Mathematical modelling is an iterative process that requires students to move back and forth between the four components in the mathematical modelling process. The students must move between the contextualized setting of the problem and the decontextualized setting of the problem.

The diagram below represents mathematical modelling. The diagram identifies and numbers the four components. The numbers do not indicate steps, but rather emphasize the key categories captured within the mathematical modelling process. Each of the four components—understanding the problem, analyzing the situation, creating a mathematical model, and analyzing and assessing the model—are comprised of many smaller aspects.

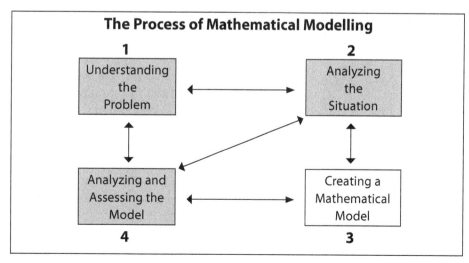

The Process of Mathematical Modelling

1. Understanding the Problem
2. Analyzing the Situation
3. Creating a Mathematical Model
4. Analyzing and Assessing the Model

This chapter will highlight the component, analyzing the situation, of mathematical modelling. I will identify the component, detail the roles of teachers and students, and share student work samples, to demonstrate student thinking within the component. The chapter will conclude with real-world problem examples for each grade level—primary, elementary and intermediate—so that you can participate in mathematical modelling and examine each problem from the perspective of analyzing the situation.

What's Involved in Analyzing the Situation

In the component, analyzing the situation, the student frames the problem and explores it within a mathematical perspective. It is during this process that the student mathematizes their thinking. Consider it from your perspective. When you encounter a problem in the real world, it is often messy and complex. To be able to approach it, you have to understand it (the first component of mathematical modelling). Once you understand the problem, it is now expected that you refine it so that it can be solved.

From the perspective of mathematical modelling, the student needs to take the necessary time to refine the real-world problem. In refining the problem, the student makes it workable. The student has framed the problem in a way to find a suitable approach and reach a meaningful solution.

To be able to refine the problem, the student must make one or more assumptions (Butler Wolf, 2015; Wickstrom & Aytes, 2018). The assumption(s) made by students can be based on their lived experiences, their understanding of the context within the problem, and their preferences in a similar situation. Typically, students will make assumptions based on something that is important to the real-world problem. Students will decide what they will keep and what they will ignore in the problem. The work that students take in analyzing the situation leads to an idealized version of the original real-world problem.

In addition to basing assumptions on lived experiences, students can also make assumptions based on curriculum, or subject areas. However, many students will rely on mathematics for making assumptions. This could be because they are engaged in mathematical modelling and/or because the teacher has crafted a learning environment that consciously or subconsciously stresses mathematics as being the basis of assumptions.

Students will make assumptions to refine the parameters of the problem. Once assumptions are made, students will idealize the situation by identifying conditions. The assumptions make the problem manageable so that students can work within certain parameters. Conditions, as well as assumptions, make the problem manageable. Conditions can be made to provide limitations and restrictions within the real-world problem. Both assumptions and conditions provide structure to the messy, ill-defined problem.

Questions that students can ask themselves or others when working within this component are:

- What assumptions can I make regarding this situation?
- How can I make this situation workable? What changes? What stays the same?

Before we look at the roles of the teacher and student in analyzing the situation, it must be noted that making assumptions may or may not come easily

Assumption(s) made by students can be based on their lived experiences, their understanding of the context within the problem, and their references in a similar situation.

to students. Remember back to our discussion on how students have typically encountered defined problems in mathematics. Well, when having to make assumptions, students must take an independent role in their learning. This can be, and most likely is, a foreign experience for students. So, we must be cognizant that the ability to make one or more assumption cannot be taken for granted.

The Teacher's Role

Although it is the student who will be making the assumption(s), either individually or collaboratively with other students, the teacher does play a significant role. Students have not had many experiences in making assumptions. I say this, because many students have spent much of their time in mathematics working through defined problems where students are not required to make assumptions. As such, the ability to read a problem, understand it, and then analyze it to make a suitable assumption may be challenging for students.

Teachers can support students in making assumptions through questioning. Questioning is a facilitating skill. It means that the teacher must listen to how students communicate their understanding of the problem and then ask them questions about their understanding. This technique can support students in working through stumbling blocks and lead them to make assumptions. The teacher relies on both content knowledge and mathematical modelling knowledge to craft questions. Avoid leading questions otherwise it is the teachers who are doing the thinking and not the students.

In addition to supporting students in crafting individual assumptions, teachers can also use questioning to assist students in working through the selection of assumptions to make the real-world problem workable. When students are working collaboratively, there may be more than one assumption generated. In such a case, the teacher can use questioning to inspire students to move beyond the simplistic comparison of the assumptions. The comparison should be one that is based on the context of the real-world problem and that is structured on the review of how such assumptions can implicate the problem moving forward.

When thinking about the implication of the assumption, the teacher can ask students to consider how the mathematization of the real-world problem can influence the mathematical model created and the possible solution. The assumption that students select to idealize the real-world problem has a significant impact on the work to come later in the problem. The assumption provides the parameters of the work and instills a restriction in the problem that can make it applicable to be framed within a mathematical model.

Once an assumption has been made, the teacher can ask students to make their assumption explicit. When students explicitly state their assumption, they are clarifying their understanding of the real-world problem and stating how they determined the specific assumption. It is during this recount that students investigate the suitability of their assumption to the problem. And, in a manner of supporting classroom discourse, having students share their assumptions provides the opportunity for all students to hear the assumptions made by others. Allowing students to share their assumptions with the class will assist in later use when they find themselves working through real-world problems in the future.

Consider the following teachers' comments about their roles during mathematical modelling. The comments refer to the second component—analyzing the situation—of mathematical modelling.

> Teachers can ask students to consider how the mathematization of the real-world problem can influence the mathematical model created and the possible solution.

Honestly, I thought that this would be the most straightforward part of the math modelling. I was wrong. Students didn't feel comfortable with making assumptions that could shape the problem. They felt as though this wasn't math.

When working through this part of mathematical modelling, I had to do a lot of facilitation with my students. I had to do a shared activity where we would craft assumptions as a class. In fact, even after that, students didn't feel comfortable in making assumptions that would make the problem manageable. The assumptions they did make would do little to move the problem forward.

Making assumptions took a lot of time for our students. There was much debate between students in deciding which assumptions would be best for the problem. If students had alternative thoughts on what the assumption(s) should be, there was lots of debate. Much of the rationale given by students in supporting their assumption was based on the preferences of students.

The teacher can provide opportunities to strengthen the ability of students to make assumptions. One approach to such work can be to provide students with a mathematical model and ask students what assumptions must have been made to the real-world problem to make it suitable for this model. This approach may seem counterintuitive to students being independent learners since it is the teacher modelling the process. However, there is a level of independence that students need to demonstrate. For one, students must critically examine the real-world problem and the mathematical model to determine the assumptions to make this transition happen. Such critical examination is a necessary skill that students must possess to be an independent learner. What the teacher is doing in this situation is crafting an experience that focuses on the thinking necessary to make assumptions. This experience can then be applied by the student when working through the mathematical modelling process.

The Student's Role

Applying assumptions to the problem will establish parameters that acts as a form of mathematization.

Analyzing the situation involves the students taking the real-world problem and applying assumptions to it so that it is workable and has a structure. Applying assumptions to the problem will establish parameters that acts as a form of mathematization. While still working with the problem in a contextualized setting, the student must make assumptions so that there are established parameters representing the problem within a mathematical model.

This math modelling process allows students to refine the real-world problem. By refining the problem in a contextualized setting, students can address the lack of structure in the ill-defined problem. Once this is accomplished students can work toward a meaningful solution. By making assumptions, students are ensuring that the model developed is realistic and appropriate to the original problem presented (Stohlmann & Albarracin, 2016).

When engaging in analyzing the situation, there are certain skills that students need to possess such as critical thinking, engagement, confidence, and patience. When reviewing the real-world problem and their understanding of it, students must think about what assumptions must be made to provide a structure to the problem. Students need to think critically of their lived experiences, the context within the problem, and mathematics that could be applied. It is not as easy as picking an assumption out of the dark. Much thought goes into making an assumption that correctly fits the situation and will lead to a workable process.

During the analysis of the situation, students must engage in the mathematical modelling process. This cannot be surface level. Students must reflect on the real-world problem, the context in which it is presented, and the thinking that they bring to the situation. If students are not engaged, meaningful opportunities will be missed in crafting a workable problem.

Confidence is a necessity in mathematical modelling. Analyzing the situation requires the students to approach the real-world problem and their understanding of the problem from a perspective of confidence. Students, when confident, can make assumptions and can communicate these with others. Without confidence, students will be hesitant to interact with the contextualized real-world problem. Without confidence, students are at the risk of not completing the mathematical modelling process. An inability to make sense of a problem and to make assumptions will make the process more difficult when faced with stumbling blocks.

Much like other aspects of mathematical modelling, analyzing the situation requires patience. Very rarely will students glide through the work when engaged with real-world problems. Instead, students need to be patient and recognize that when one attempt does not lead to a successful solution, they can learn from this experience and make better informed decisions next time. Patience is an important skill all students should possess so they do not make decisions in haste and quit. Patience will assist with going through iterations of mathematical modelling in finding a solution.

Consider the following comments students provided to describe their approach in analyzing the situation.

Confidence is a necessity in mathematical modelling.

PRIMARY EXAMPLE: A STUDENT EXPLAINS

I love it that I can make assumptions when solving problems. I can use what I know in math to make an assumption, and I can use my life experiences to make assumptions. I just got to remember that my assumptions have to make sense and that the assumptions will change what counts as an answer for the problem.

It's hard to know what assumptions to make when analyzing the situation. Sometimes I have an assumption that I think is good when another person has a different assumption. It can be hard to know which assumption to use.

When I work on understanding the problem, you can easily recognize if you're right or wrong. However, when making an assumption, you're not sure if it's a good one or not. And sometimes it's really hard to make an assumption because you don't have any experience with the type of thing being discussed in the problem.

Making assumptions is a challenging task for students. It requires students to make connections with the real-world problem. These connections can be based on either the student's mathematical understanding or their life experiences. Making assumptions is a part of the mathematization process whereby students need to take autonomy in their learning. Autonomy is a form of independence and influences how students will work through mathematical modelling.

Student Work Samples

Let's explore the component, analyzing the situation, in action. We will review the work samples from a primary, elementary, and intermediate student. For each work sample, I will share the real-world problem, highlight aspects of student thinking and the facilitation questions that teachers asked the students as they were engaged with the task.

Primary

The following problem was assigned to primary students.

> The Kindergarten classroom recognized that many of their supplies for centres were needing to be replaced. The teacher shared that they needed to buy new supplies but that they had a limited budget.

The table highlights the primary student's thinking as they analyze with the situation.

What assumptions can I make regarding this situation?

- Kindergarten classrooms use certain kinds of things.
- The supplies would have to not break easily.
- There would have to be different kinds of supplies so that Kindergarten students have choices in what to play with.

- When supplies were selected, there would have to be enough for more than one person to use at a time.

How can I make this situation workable? What changes? What stays the same?

- Limit the number of supplies.
- Based on the number of supplies, the budget may go up or down.
- Think about the things we liked to play with when we were in Kindergarten so it is not too many choices.

The following table highlights the questions the primary teacher asked as they were facilitating students analyzing the situation.

TEACHER FACILITATION QUESTIONS

- How did you decide on the types of supplies to buy?
- About how many supplies will you need?
- When you were working through understanding the real-world problem, you identified information you need to know. Have you made any decisions regarding that missing information?

Elementary

The following problem was assigned to elementary students.

> *The local elementary school was selected as the site for the cross-country meet. As part of holding this meet, the school had to decide how to accommodate people wanting to watch the meet.*

The table highlights the elementary student's thinking as they analyze the situation.

STUDENT THINKING

What assumptions can I make regarding this situation?

- Usually athletes can only have 3–4 guests attend a session.
- The cross-country team usually has 20 athletes for both boys and girls.
- The race is around the school property.

How can I make this situation workable? What changes? What stays the same?

- Depending on the number of athletes, the number of attendees will change. If there are more athletes, there are more attendees. If there are less athletes, there are less attendees.

- The ratio of athletes to attendees remains the same.
- Depending on the location of the race, the amount of space for attendees can be altered.

The following table highlights the questions the elementary teacher asked as they were facilitating students analyzing the situation.

TEACHER FACILITATION QUESTIONS

- What do you know about cross-country teams?
- Does any of this problem seem familiar to you? Can you make any connections to it?
- How many people have you seen at a school sports event before?
- When you were working through understanding the real-world problem, you identified information you need to know. Have you made any decisions regarding that missing information?

Intermediate

The following problem was assigned to intermediate students.

> *In planning end-of-year activities, the school administration decide that the Grade 8 students would go on a field trip. The administration wanted to know what the cost per student would be for such a trip.*

The table highlights the intermediate student's thinking as they analyze the situation.

STUDENT THINKING

What assumptions can I make regarding this situation?

- The field trip is one day.
- No need to pay for accommodations.
- Students will pay for a portion of the trip.
- Chaperones will pay for their own food.

How can I make this situation workable? What changes? What stays the same?

- With the field trip being one day, we can remove the consideration of hotels. If the trip goes beyond a day, the price of a hotel needs to be included.
- Chaperones paying for their food will lower the cost per student. This cost per student will increase if students have to cover the cost of chaperone meals.
- If the school decides to not pay for a portion of the field trip, students will have to pay more.

The following table highlights the questions of the intermediate teacher asked as they were facilitating students analyzing the situation.

Anticipating Classroom Connections

We have reviewed some real-world problems, the student thinking process of analyzing the situation, and questions from the teacher to facilitate student learning. Now, let's revisit the same three problems introduced at the end of Chapter 4. You will need to consider is how you have already engaged in understanding the problem. In each problem, consider the following:

- Anticipate how students will answer the four following questions:
  - What assumptions can I make regarding this situation?
  - How can I make this situation workable? What changes? What stays the same?
- Consider facilitation questions that you can have in your repertoire to support student analysis of the situation.

Primary Real-World Problem

Consider the following real-world problem assigned to primary students:

You are planning to have a birthday party and would like to give everyone a gift bag as they leave. How much will this cost?

Elementary Real-World Problem

Consider the following real-world problem assigned to elementary students:

As a way to store items that students play with while on the playground, the leadership group decided to build storage bins. The principal agreed to this so long as the cost of the project was effectively managed.

Intermediate Real-World Problem

Consider the following real-world problem assigned to intermediate students:

The population of your community is growing. There are already limited housing options available to current residents. What can the community do?

Summary

Being able to make assumptions will translate a real-world problem into a workable problem.

Throughout the chapter, I have stressed the role that making assumptions plays in the mathematical modelling process. Being able to make assumptions will translate a real-world problem into a workable problem. It provides structure to an ill-defined problem so that the student can craft a model that can be used to solve the problem. It is through this process of making assumptions, that students mathematize the situation and, as such, mathematize their thinking.

Since the mathematical modelling process is iterative, students will go back and forth between the first and second components of the mathematical modelling process. Within a contextualized setting, students make sense of a real-world problem and structure it so that mathematics can be applied.

When students are analyzing the situation, they are making assumptions that will frame the ill-defined problem. The assumptions that students make will influence the outcome of their work. Assumptions will influence the parameter of the problem and will influence the solutions that are meaningful to the original question. Students must be aware that such assumptions are influenced by their mathematical knowledge and their lived experiences. This is why, much like it is in the real world, the mathematical modelling process is dependent on the knowledge and experiences that students bring with them to understand the messy real-world problem.

The analyzing the situation component of mathematical modelling may be something relatively new for students. When working with defined problems, many of the problems that students are assigned over the years, they are not required to make assumptions. Not being familiar with making assumptions may impact the level of confidence and independence students have when working within these mathematical modelling components. Therefore, teachers will need to apply their facilitating skills so that students can be guided through making assumptions.

Mathematical modelling is an iterative process that requires students to be independent and critical thinkers. Students who are capable and confident math learners make assumptions that support their work in solving the problem. Assumptions provide structure to ill-defined problems and will create parameters through which future work will be based upon.

6

Creating a Mathematical Model

The mathematical modelling process continues with the component, creating a mathematical model. To move back and forth between the four components, students must move between the contextualized setting of the problem and the decontextualized setting of the problem.

The diagram below represents mathematical modelling. The diagram identifies and numbers each of the components. We have reviewed two of the components in Chapters 4 and 5 so now let's continue with the next component, creating a mathematical model.

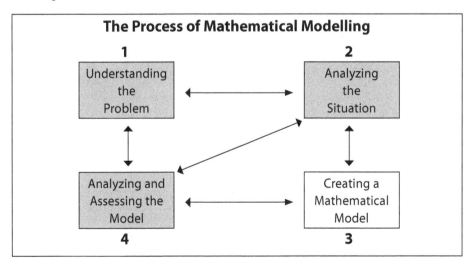

The Process of Mathematical Modelling

1		2
Understanding the Problem	↔	Analyzing the Situation
Analyzing and Assessing the Model	↔	Creating a Mathematical Model
4		3

The chapter will cover an overview of the component, detail the roles of teachers and students, and share student work samples, to demonstrate student thinking within the component. Similar to Chapters 4 and 5, we will finish the chapter with the same real-world problem examples so you can participate in mathematical modelling and examine the problem from the perspective discussed in this chapter.

What's Involved in Creating a Mathematical Model

This component of the mathematical modelling process, creating a mathematical model, is where students move from a contextualized approach to thinking in a mathematical perspective. Students work within a decontextualized setting during this component. As students move from a contextualized to decontextualized setting, they translate the idealized version of the problem into mathematical terms. From this translation, students will obtain a mathematical formulation of the idealized question. This formulation is the mathematical model.

When students decontextualize the problem through mathematics, they take the time to examine the structured problem, based on their work from the previous two components (understanding the problem and analyzing the situation). By making assumptions and identifying conditions, students can now approach the problem from a mathematical perspective. Students will decide on the mathematical language and concepts to apply, and the method to take.

When creating a mathematical model, students have the freedom to explore and select the mathematical concept used to frame the work (Butler Wolf, 2015; Wickstrom & Aytes, 2018). As mentioned throughout this book, an important aspect of mathematical modelling is students being independent. Students explore the problem from a mathematical perspective, select the concept that represents the problem, and based on their understanding of the real-world problem, make the required assumptions. The result will be creating multiple options for both the solution pathway and the solution itself.

During this component of the mathematical modelling process students not only create a model but also work through it to reach a solution. Working through the solution can be done through numerical calculations, concrete representations, pictures, graphical analysis, and so on. This solution is still to be considered only from a mathematical perspective. It is also considered within a decontextualized setting. The analysis of the solution depends on whether the mathematical procedure is applied accurately based upon mathematical principles.

Questions that students can ask themselves or others when working within this component are:

- What mathematical language and concepts can the student apply to the now structured problem?
- What representations and supports can the student apply to build a mathematical model?

Before moving onto the roles of the teachers and students in creating a mathematical model, it must be documented that students may have difficulty selecting the best mathematical approach to solve the problem. Having such freedom may be overwhelming to some students. What should be noted, however, is that

When creating a mathematical model, students have the freedom to explore and select the mathematical concept used to frame the work.

the more opportunities students are given to explore and select mathematical approaches when solving a problem, the more confidence and independence they will gain.

The Teacher's Role

The more opportunities students are given to explore and select mathematical approaches when solving a problem, the more confidence and independence they will gain.

Students have the freedom to explore and select mathematical concepts that will best be able to frame the idealized problem they formed. It is through this exploration that students can consider how best to reach a solution that addresses the real-world problem and assumptions they made. While it is the student's choice in selecting the math concept to use as the basis of creating a mathematical model, teachers play a significant role in making this happen.

Consider the following teacher's comments about their roles during mathematical modelling. The comments refer to the third component—creating a mathematical model—of mathematical modelling.

PRIMARY EXAMPLE: A TEACHER EXPLAINS

Of all the parts of mathematical modelling, this is the part that I'm most comfortable in supporting. It's similar to most of the math experiences that I had as a student and the math experiences I have crafted for my students in the past. It came as a surprise that students struggled with this. Many wanted me to direct them on the best way to frame their mathematical thinking.

ELEMENTARY EXAMPLE: A TEACHER EXPLAINS

When I was starting with the math modelling process, I thought that this would be the most straightforward for students. While it focuses on the math concepts that we have explored in class, what I didn't consider was the choice that students would need to make during this component. Some of my students weren't sure which representation to use to solve the problem. They became overwhelmed with the choice.

INTERMEDIATE EXAMPLE: A TEACHER EXPLAINS

When students were creating a mathematical model, they tended to select math concepts that we just recently studied in class. I'm not sure if it was because these concepts were fresh on students' minds or if it was because students forgot concepts they studied earlier in the year. I had to facilitate a lot of conversations to support students in selecting a mathematical concept that would align with the problem and assumptions they made.

From the comments we can see that the teachers can assist students in working through this component of mathematical modelling. The teachers revealed that their students struggled to create a mathematical model. Whether it was students wanting the teacher to make the decision for them, students being overwhelmed with the number of options, or students relying on mathematical concepts only recently studied in class, students relied on the teacher to support them in creating a mathematical model for the idealized problem. This is not the outcome we are looking to achieve with our students.

One approach teachers can take in supporting students is to use questions to move students toward independent thinking. Asking the following questions would provide students opportunities to question their thinking and consider options for moving forward:

- What pictures, diagrams, or graphs might help people understand your information, model, and results?
- How can you organize your data to share with an individual unfamiliar with your project?

The first question encourages students to frame possibilities for their model and to consider a way to support understanding of their work. The second question encourages students to consider options for organizing their work so that people who have not invested the time that they have in the problem can make meaning with their work.

Continuing to support students in creating a mathematical model, the teacher can inspire students to consider more than one mathematical concept to frame the model. For example, the teacher can encourage students to consider two or three approaches to creating a model and compare the results. By remaining open to selecting different mathematical concepts, students have time to consider additional approaches to creating a mathematical model and to select tools that provide more insight into the problem. It is during this comparison of models that students can identify the model that is better suited for the idealized problem they crafted within the first two mathematical modelling components.

Teachers played the role of facilitator within the first two components of the mathematical modelling process, and this role continues in the third component. Students may encounter stumbling blocks when they are expected to select a mathematical concept to frame their work in this decontextualized setting of the mathematical modelling process. This concept that students select is the basis for how they will reach a mathematical solution for the idealized question they crafted from the real-world problem. Teachers can facilitate students through the creation of mathematical model by using questions and by offering students the opportunity to compare various models that could be used in reaching a solution.

The Student's Role

Having the autonomy to select the mathematical model empowers students to take initiative in solving the problem and making meaning.

Creating a mathematical model requires students to have a good understanding of the idealized question they have crafted from the initial real-world problem they encountered. This idealized question, formed within a contextualized setting, now has the structure that it can be explored and solved using mathematics. It is up to the students to determine the mathematical concept which the mathematical model is based upon.

Having the autonomy to select the mathematical model empowers students to take initiative in solving the problem and making meaning. Over time, students should become able to choose a concept as the basis of the mathematical model. This concept can be a **concrete representation**, **visual representation**, **numerical representation**, and so on. However, over time, students should be expected to apply more sophisticated tools and representations to create and solve their mathematical models. This can be attributed to the increased confidence students have in mathematical modelling and their experiences to dig deeper into mathematical concepts and explore new concepts.

Within this third component of the mathematical modelling process, students are not only expected to create a mathematical model but also to solve it. Once students have identified a concept to use as the basis of their created mathematical model, students then work through the model and reach a solution. It is expected that students work through the mathematical model accurately and arrive at a solution without error. A key point to remember, however, is that this work of creating a model and working it through to a solution is done within a decontextualized setting. Concrete objects, visuals, and numbers are applied within the model from the perspective of mathematics not from the context of the initial real-world problem students encountered. The focus of working through the model is to accurately apply the mathematical concept. It is not about considering the context of the initial real-world problem. It is about applying the mathematical model within the idealized question, based on the understanding and assumptions of students.

Once students have created a mathematical model and reached a solution, students should then be able to communicate their work in terms of the idealized question and how they created the model and solved it. At the conclusion of this, students will be able to form conclusions about the mathematical model and its effectiveness in reaching a solution of the idealized question within a decontextualized setting. Students can compare and contrast the mathematical model they created and their ability to reach a solution.

In the work of creating a mathematical model, students need to have confidence and perseverance. Confidence is needed in determining which mathematical concept to use as the basis of the mathematical model. Students can become overwhelmed with the options available when creating a model, but they will come to believe in themselves and in their ability to make an appropriate choice. The key is to believe in their mathematical understanding. Students may have to return to the drawing board in terms of selecting a concept for their mathematical model to persevere. Since this is an iterative process, it will require students to not only restart a component but to go back and forth between components. Students must acknowledge this as an integral aspect of mathematical modelling and embrace it. Perseverance will get them through these challenges.

Consider the following comments students provided to describe their approach in creating a mathematical model.

> **Confidence is needed in determining which mathematical concept to use as the basis of the mathematical model. Students can become overwhelmed with the options available when creating a model.**

PRIMARY EXAMPLE: A STUDENT EXPLAINS

After we understand the problem and make decisions about what to include it in, we have to create a mathematical model. The questions that the teacher gave us to help us make the choice is really, really, helpful. I use the question to pick the best math topic to make the model.

ELEMENTARY EXAMPLE: A STUDENT EXPLAINS

I find it hard to pick a concept to use as my mathematical model. Once I have it, I can do the work. I just don't know which one is the best.

This is the math that I am good at. The only thing I wish was different was that the teacher provided more direction for which math concept to use to create the mathematical model. There are too many options that I can choose from. It can be a bit much sometimes.

Creating a mathematical model can be a challenging task for students. They must examine the idealized question they formed, based on their understanding of the original real-world problem and their assumptions, against mathematical concepts. This examination is completed within a decontextualized setting. It can be an overwhelming choice for students since they select one concept to use as the mathematical model.

Student Work Samples

Let us turn to the work samples from students from each level as we have done in other chapters. Each work sample is an example of primary, elementary, and intermediate work. Now that we are focusing on the creating a mathematical model we will highlight aspects of student thinking and the facilitation questions that teachers asked students as they created a mathematical model.

Primary

The following problem was assigned to primary students.

The Kindergarten classroom recognized that many of their supplies for centres were needing to be replaced. The teacher shared that they needed to buy new supplies but that they had a limited budget.

The table highlights the primary student's thinking as they create a mathematical model.

STUDENT THINKING

What mathematical language and concepts can be applied to the now structured problem?

- Surveys
- Lists
- Ordering likes
- Addition of prices

What representations and supports can be used to build a mathematical model?

- Pictures to list items
- Numbers for prices

The following table highlights the questions the primary teacher asked as they were facilitating students creating a mathematical model.

TEACHER FACILITATION QUESTIONS
• What math can you see in the problem? • What concept can help you make sense of this problem? • How could you explain your thinking to others?

Elementary

The following problem was assigned to elementary students.

The local elementary school was selected as the site for the cross-country meet. As part of holding this meet, the school had to decide how to accommodate people wanting to watch the meet.

The table highlights the elementary student's thinking as they create a mathematical model.

STUDENT THINKING
What mathematical language and concepts can be applied to the now structured problem? • Multiplication • Ratio • Perimeter **What representations and supports can be used to build a mathematical model?** • Visual representation of the course • Numbers to find the total number of attendees

The following table highlights the questions the elementary teacher asked as they were facilitating students creating a mathematical model.

TEACHER FACILITATION QUESTIONS
• What pictures or diagrams could help you understand this problem? • How will you organize your data? • What concepts can support a solution to this problem?

Intermediate

The following problem was assigned to intermediate students.

> *In planning end-of-year activities, the school administration decide that the Grade 8 students would go on a field trip. The administration wanted to know what the cost per student would be for such a trip.*

The table highlights the intermediate student's thinking as they create a mathematical model.

STUDENT THINKING

What mathematical language and concepts can be applied to the now structured problem?

- Price of items
- Schedule
- Budget
- Survey

What representations and supports can be used to build a mathematical model?

- Numbers
- Spreadsheet

The following table highlights the questions the intermediate teacher asked as they were facilitating students creating a mathematical model.

TEACHER FACILITATION QUESTIONS

- What is involved in planning a trip?
- What math concepts would help you finalize plans for the trip?
- How would you organize your data?

Anticipating Classroom Connections

In the previous sections of the chapter, we have reviewed an example of a real-world problem, student thinking as they engaged with the creating a mathematical model component, and questions asked by the teacher to facilitate student learning. Next, we will revisit the real-world problems explored in Chapters 4 and 5. So, what you will need to do is consider how you have already engaged in understanding the problem and analyzing the situation that led to the forming of an idealized question. For each problem, consider the following:

- What mathematical language and concepts can the student apply to the now structured problem?
- What representations and supports can the student apply to build a mathematical model?
- What pictures, diagrams, or graphs might help people understand your information, model, and results?
- How can you organize your data to share with an individual unfamiliar with your project?

Primary Real-World Problem

Consider the following real-world problem assigned to primary students:

You are planning to have a birthday party and would like to give everyone a gift bag as they leave. How much will this cost?

Elementary Real-World Problem

Consider the following real-world problem assigned to elementary students:

As a way to store items that students play with while on the playground, the leadership group decided to build storage bins. The principal agreed to this so long as the cost of the project was effectively managed.

Intermediate Real-World Problem

Consider the following real-world problem assigned to intermediate students:

The population of your community is growing. There are already limited housing options available to current residents. What can the community do?

Summary

Within this chapter, I have emphasized the role of creating a mathematical model in the mathematical modelling process. Being able to create a mathematical model will enable students to apply mathematics to the idealized question within a decontextualized setting. Applying mathematics within such a setting allows the student to focus solely on mathematics. It is an opportunity for students to work through a model and determine if a solution can be reached without considering it in relation to the context of the original real-world problem.

And to clarify, this third component of the mathematical modelling process is not just about creating a mathematical model but also about working through it to reach a solution. It is an important consideration as before the model can be applied to the original real-world problem, the student must confirm that it is applicable to solving the idealized question based on their understanding and assumptions of the real-world problem.

Creating a mathematical model shares similarities with solving defined problems. For both, students must determine a concept to apply to the problem and then decide on how this concept will be represented within the work. It is the responsibility of the student to determine if their work is accurate and addresses the question being asked. Where it differs is that in the mathematical modelling process, students are not finished the problem when completing this process. Instead, students must move to the fourth component of mathematical modelling that requires them to analyze and assess their model against the original real-world problem.

7

Analyzing and Assessing the Mathematical Model

We have reviewed three of the mathematical modelling components and now we are exploring the last one, analyzing and assessing the model. Throughout the chapters we now see how unique this process is in developing students' confidence and giving them the skills to understand and frame real-world problems.

The diagram below represents mathematical modelling. We are now at the fourth component of the mathematical modelling process.

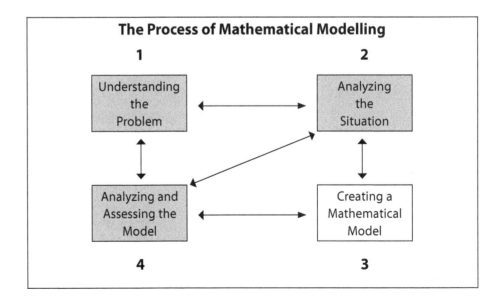

The Process of Mathematical Modelling

1
Understanding the Problem

2
Analyzing the Situation

4
Analyzing and Assessing the Model

3
Creating a Mathematical Model

The fourth component, analyzing and assessing the model, is when students return to thinking of the problem within a contextualized setting. They analyze the mathematical model against the original real-world problem, assess the model's ability to solve this problem, and then draw conclusions based on the responses they have crafted. Within this, I will provide an overview of the component, detail the roles of teachers and students, and share student work samples to demonstrate student thinking within the component. We will then conclude the chapter by reviewing the same real-world problems one final time.

What's Involved in Analyzing and Assessing the Model

When students are engaged with defined problems, the calculated solution tends to be the final step in the problem-solving process. Students will work through their thinking toward a solution and will reflect upon their work. When engaged with ill-defined problems within the mathematical modelling process, students must interpret their solution and compare it against the contextualized real-world problem. Engaging in such an interpretation is referred to as the analyzing and assessing the model component of the mathematical modelling process. It is during this component that students leave behind the decontextualized setting of creating a mathematical model to re-enter the contextualized setting of the original real-world problem they were assigned to solve.

As students have framed the real-world problem within an idealized question, using assumptions and approximations, a critical aspect of analyzing and assessing the model must be to assess the ability of the mathematical model to satisfy the demands presented within the original real-world problem. To undertake an analysis and assessment of the model, students must first interpret the results of the mathematical model in terms of the original real-world problem. From this interpretation, students will then validate the approach by comparing it with the contextualized aspects of the real-world problem. Students will draw conclusions based on this work and will report their findings to others. It is necessary that within this reporting, others can easily recognize the many decisions made by students during the mathematical modelling process and can identify ways to replicate this work themselves if need be.

The mathematical modelling process takes students away from the real-world problem that they first encounter. As students work to make the problem applicable to mathematics, they make assumptions and approximations to create parameters of the real-world problem. From there, students will then consider this idealized question from a decontextualized, mathematical perspective where they will create a model and work toward a solution. As students progress through these components, they are taken away from the real-world problem posed at the onset of the experience. This removal from the original real-world problem may make it difficult for the students to remain connected to the context of the problem. Therefore, during the analyzing and assessing the model component, students re-engage with the contextualized setting of the problem. They interpret the solution and compare it to the context that frames the real-world problem. And, during this re-engagement with context, students increase their depth of understanding which enables them to identify strengths and weaknesses within their work. Doing so, students will remove the barriers between the world they live in and the mathematics within the classroom (Butler Wolf, 2015).

> It is necessary that within this reporting, others can easily recognize the many decisions made by students during the mathematical modelling process and can identify ways to replicate this work themselves if need be.

When analyzing and assessing the model, students reintroduce the work they have done with the mathematical model to the context of the real-world problem. During this analysis and assessment, students question the validity of their model as it stands in reference to the real-world problem, the assumptions they made and the conditions they have identified. Students will determine if their mathematical model provides a reasonable solution to the real-world problem and whether alternative models exist. Exploring possibilities for alternative models will strengthen the student's ability to understand the real-world problem and how crafting an idealized question (based upon understanding the problem and making assumptions and approximations) can lead to situations whereby other models are possible.

Questions that students can ask themselves or others when working within this component:

- Does my mathematical model lead to a reasonable solution to the problem?
- Do alternative mathematical models exist?

Before moving onto the discussion of the teacher's and student's role in analyzing and assessing the model, it must be emphasized that when students work through this component, their work may not be finished. Since this is an iterative process, students may have to return to one of the other three components to adjust their thinking. Analyzing and assessing the model does not mean students are wrapping up with the mathematical modelling process; they may identify misconceptions in their work, whether it be in their understanding of the real-world problem, how they crafted an idealized question from this contextualized problem, and/or the mathematical model they crafted and employed. In reality, analyzing and assessing the model may lead students to a conclusion or take them back to the first component of the mathematical modelling process.

The Teacher's Role

This fourth component of the mathematical modelling process can take a significant amount of time for students.

Similar to the other three components of the mathematical modelling process, analyzing and assessing the model is meant to be student directed. This can be done by students working individually or working collaboratively with others. The teacher, however, plays a significant role in facilitating the component. As mentioned in the previous section, analyzing and assessing the model is not usually a focus when students work through defined problems. And, since students generally work more with defined problems than ill-defined problems, this component is sometimes either omitted or rushed by students.

As this component may not be one that students have much experience with or consider important, the teacher must demonstrate patience. This fourth component of the mathematical modelling process can take a significant amount of time for students. Students will need to re-examine their work, from the entry point of their mathematical modelling to solving the mathematical model they created in the third component. As such, the teacher needs to be patient with students and in their ability to work through this component. Perhaps providing more opportunities for conversation and collaboration among students is required. Students should have opportunities to share concerns and questions that they encounter about their analysis and assessment. Although teachers may believe that students are experiencing struggle, we cannot forget that struggle is

Teachers need to view this component as a significant learning experience for students as opposed to simply double-checking their work. Analyzing and assessing the model is about students critically examining their work.

an inherent part of the learning process (Costello, 2021). And, therefore, we will be patient and guide students through this stumbling block toward a solution that makes sense.

Another crucial element that the teacher must bring to facilitating learning as students analyze and assess the model is understanding of the mathematical modelling process. Teachers need to be fully aware of the fourth component, analyzing and assessing the model, and recognize the importance it plays in the process. Teachers need to view this component as a significant learning experience for students as opposed to simply double-checking their work. Analyzing and assessing the model is about students critically examining their work and putting their decontextualized mathematical thinking into the contextualized setting of the original problem. It is about having students feel capable and confident in communicating their thinking and considering if their work has led to a meaningful response to the real-world problem. It is an opportunity for students to both consolidate their thinking and extend their thinking for future encounters with mathematical modelling.

As a way of supporting students analyzing and assessing the model, consider the following questions that teachers could use to facilitate the mathematical modelling experience of students.

- Will your created model generate approximate or precise solutions?
- Do the results make sense to the real-world problem you initially encountered?
- In what types of contexts would your model provide important information?
- If you change the assumptions you made to the real-world problem, how much would your mathematical model and solutions change?
- Would it improve the model to change something decided at an earlier step and resolve the problem?

Consider the following teachers' comments about their roles during the fourth component of mathematical modelling, analyzing and assessing the model.

PRIMARY EXAMPLE: A TEACHER EXPLAINS

I didn't realize the amount of time that would need to be dedicated to this part of the mathematical modelling process. It isn't just checking over your work. It's about thinking through your work and reconnecting it back to the problem they were assigned. It's an in-depth thinking activity.

ELEMENTARY EXAMPLE: A TEACHER EXPLAINS

I had to guide students through analyzing and assessing their model. It wasn't something that students wanted to do initially. They thought that their work was done when they solved the mathematical model they created in the previous component. When we did start to focus on analyzing and assessing the model, they skimmed through it. We spent a lot of time talking about this part of the process needing to be thorough and reflective of all the work they did. Then, from this thinking, they needed to decide if their work was suitable and could be used to effectively solve the messy problem they were first given.

Communication, communication, communication. This is what I stressed to my students when they were analyzing and assessing the model. I wanted them to be able to clearly articulate their thinking throughout the mathematical modelling process. It was about students being able to walk others through their work and provide rationale as to why they made the decisions they did. The point of this communication is for students to be transparent when explaining their thinking. By being transparent, others could pick up where students left and apply this same model to other problems that are similar.

Teachers need to support students in moving beyond a surface level analysis and assessment.

The teacher recognizes the importance of analyzing and assessing the model. Whether it was the realization that this component takes considerable time and is more than double-checking work, or the fact that teachers need to support students in moving beyond a surface level analysis and assessment. This learning activity is something that requires students to critically reflect on their thinking and how they moved from being presented a real-world problem to mathematizing their thinking and creating a model. When working through analyzing and assessing the model, students need to understand the mathematical modelling process, mathematical concepts and representations, and the contextual elements of the real-world problem. It is the intersection between these three aspects and the ability for the student to move between a contextualized setting and decontextualized setting while navigating the mathematical modelling process that learning truly occurs.

The Student's Role

Analyzing and assessing the model requires students to have certain skills, such as critical thinking, communication, independence, and depth of knowledge. To engage in an effective analysis and assessment, the student must go back and forth between a contextual setting and a decontextualized setting. It requires students to critically examine their thinking from the onset of the mathematical modelling process to the conclusion. As such, students will have to consider much in terms of the real-world context, the mathematical concepts and representations being applied, and the mathematical modelling process itself.

When engaged in this fourth component of the mathematical modelling process, the students will have to take a step back and critically examine their work. To engage in such a critical perspective, the student will have to examine not only the work they did throughout the process but also the rationale behind each decision. Students must go beyond double-checking their work to ask:

- Why did I choose this approach?
- What are the implications of choosing this approach?
- What else could I have done instead of this approach?

Applying a critical examination of both the model and its impact will provide students with a comprehensive view of their work. It will also assist students in determining whether their work was the best option or if they should have

Students must be able to clearly communicate the many decision points within the mathematical modelling process. It is about making the implicit explicit.

selected another option for the model. When students consider the reasonableness of their model and solution, they remove the barriers between mathematics and the real world (Butler Wolf, 2015).

Along with critical thinking, communication is also of great importance. Students must be able to clearly communicate the many decision points within the mathematical modelling process. It is about making the implicit explicit. Not only does such communication support student understanding, but it also supports students in providing a transparent account of their work to others. A key aspect of the mathematical modelling process is for those not involved in the process to be able to clearly follow the thinking supporting the work and be able to replicate such an approach if desired. Thus, communication supports student understanding of their work and the ability for others to understand it.

To move through the analyzing and assessing component of the mathematical modelling process, students must have independence. It is this independence that will support students as they begin the process of investigating their model in relation to the real-world problem. Analyzing and assessing the model can be a turbulent endeavor that could lead the student back to previously explored components. This iterative process can contribute to students wanting to rely on the teacher for answers. Being independent will assist students to dig into their thinking, approach to the mathematical modelling process, and ability to communicate their thinking with others.

When students successfully navigate analyzing and assessing the model, they bring the mathematical model process to its completion. Being able to mathematically model will aid students in contributing to the production of knowledge. Students actively construct new understandings that will not only benefit them as math learners but also support the learning of others when they can share their work. The key to mathematical modelling is the generation of knowledge and understanding, which supports students in developing their higher-order thinking skills.

Consider the following comments students provided to describe their approach in analyzing and assessing the model.

PRIMARY EXAMPLE: A STUDENT EXPLAINS

Before I mostly just checked my work to see if I made any mistakes. This doesn't cut it for mathematical modelling. I had to go back and forth to see if my work made sense and if it solved the messy problem. It's a lot more thinking than I do when I work on word problems.

ELEMENTARY EXAMPLE: A STUDENT EXPLAINS

It's hard to think about the things that I did in the modelling process. When I had to analyze and assess my model, I had to go all the way back to the first part in my work and see if what I had done really answered the question I was given. I find it hard to go back and forth between the real-world problem and the math problem I created using assumptions.

I am good at working through the mathematical modelling process. I usually have success at being able to solve any type of problem that I am given. What I found challenging was to communicate my thinking within this process. I know that I have to do it so that others can see what I did and why I did it. And, by doing this, I would understand all aspects of the problem. However, I usually forget some of these steps, especially when I go back and forth between the problem in context and the problem without context.

Analyzing and assessing the model is not an add-on or extra, it is a crucial aspect of the mathematical modelling process.

Based on the comments above, it is clear that analyzing and assessing the model can be a challenging task for students. Each of the students refer to the complexity of this component, whether it is the necessity of going back and forth between contextualized settings and decontextualized settings, recounting the thinking behind the supporting work, or the volume of thought that goes into mathematical modelling. What needs to be stressed, however, is the realization that analyzing and assessing the model is not an add-on or extra, it is a crucial aspect of the mathematical modelling process that allows students to examine the validity of their work, search for alternative approaches, and share their thinking with others.

Student Work Samples

Let us review the work of the students who have been analyzing and assessing the model. For each work sample, I will share the real-world problem, highlight aspects of student thinking in relation to analyzing and assessing the model and the types of facilitation questions the teachers asked students.

Primary

The following problem was assigned to primary students.

> The Kindergarten classroom recognized that many of their supplies for centres were needing to be replaced. The teacher shared that they needed to buy new supplies but that they had a limited budget.

The table highlights the primary student's thinking as they analyzed and assessed the model.

STUDENT THINKING

Does my mathematical model lead to a reasonable solution to the problem?

- Using a survey as the model helped choose the supplies that Kindergarten students would want. It made sense.
- I used prices of the supplies to figure out how many supplies I could buy.
- I asked teachers what they normally get for money to buy supplies.

Do other alternative mathematical models exist?

- I don't know if another model exists. Maybe I could have looked at the supplies the classroom has and replaced the supplies that were getting old. That would allow me to find supplies that students like.
- This would have been more hands-on objects than the numbers I used in my model.

The following table highlights the questions the primary teacher asked as they were facilitating students analyzing and assessing the model.

TEACHER FACILITATION QUESTIONS

- Will your model get you an estimated solution or exact solutions?
- Do the results make sense to the real-world problem?

Elementary

The following problem was assigned to elementary students.

> The local elementary school was selected as the site for the cross-country meet. As part of holding this meet, the school had to decide how to accommodate people wanting to watch the meet.

The table highlights the elementary student's thinking as they analyzed and assessed the model.

STUDENT THINKING

Does my mathematical model lead to a reasonable solution to the problem?

- I did some research and found out the number of athletes that have been on cross-country teams for the last five years.
- I use a ratio to determine that for each athlete four people could attend.
- Then, I drew a picture of the school property and marked the track. I counted how many people could fit using icons. One stick figure for each person.

Do other alternative mathematical models exist?

- I don't know if any other models exist.

The following table highlights the questions the elementary teacher asked as they were facilitating students analyzing and assessing the model.

- If you change the assumptions you made to the real-world problem, how much would your mathematical model and solutions change?
- Would it improve the model to change something decided at an earlier step and resolve the problem?

Intermediate

The following problem was assigned to intermediate students.

In planning end-of-year activities, the school administration decide that the Grade 8 students would go on a field trip. The administration wanted to know what the cost per student would be for such a trip.

The table highlights the intermediate student's thinking as they analyzed and assessed the model.

STUDENT THINKING

Does my mathematical model lead to a reasonable solution to the problem?

- I decided that the trip would be one-day in length, meaning that it would be approximately 8 hours. I thought that the school wouldn't want to spend too much time traveling. I looked at local attractions and chose one that fit the age group.
- I then found the cost to go to the attraction.
- I thought of other costs: meals and travel.

Do other alternative mathematical models exist?

- I could have started with a reasonable cost, based on past field trips, and then determined if any local options were available.

The following table highlights the questions of the intermediate teacher asked as they were facilitating students analyzing and assessing the model.

TEACHER FACILITATION QUESTIONS

- Do the results make sense to the real-world problem?
- Would it improve the model to change something decided at an earlier step and resolve the problem?

Anticipating Classroom Connections

The previous section of this chapter provided an example of a real-world problem, student thinking as they engaged with the analyzing and assessing the model component, and questions asked by the teacher to facilitate student learning. Now, I will share the same three real-world problems used at the end of Chapters 4, 5, and 6. So, what you will need to do is consider how you have already engaged in understanding the problem, analyzing the situation, and creating a mathematical model. For each problem, consider the following:

- Does the mathematical model created by the student(s) lead to a reasonable solution to the problem?
- Do other alternative mathematical models exist?

Primary Real-World Problem

Consider the following real-world problem assigned to primary students:

> *You are planning to have a birthday party and would like to give everyone a gift bag as they leave. How much will this cost?*

Elementary Real-World Problem

Consider the following real-world problem assigned to elementary students:

> *As a way to store items that students play with while on the playground, the leadership group decided to build storage bins. The principal agreed to this so long as the cost of the project was effectively managed.*

Intermediate Real-World Problem

Consider the following real-world problem assigned to intermediate students:

> *The population of your community is growing. There are already limited housing options available to current residents. What can the community do?*

Summary

Students must not only recount what they did during the modelling process, they must also be able to rationalize their thinking and consider how their decisions have shaped the result.

This chapter provided an overview of the fourth component in the mathematical modelling process, analyzing and assessing the model. This component is not anything that students would have engaged with in situations prior to ill-defined problems and mathematical modelling. Typically, a student's engagement with a problem ends when they determine a solution. Students may, however, double-check their work to see if it is reasonable based on the question asked in the problem. Analyzing and assessing the model goes beyond this straightforward approach.

When engaging in analysis and assessment of the model, students have to critically examine their thinking from the onset of the mathematical modelling process. It requires students to make the implicit explicit. Students must not only recount what they did during the modelling process, they must also be able to rationalize their thinking and consider how their decisions have shaped the result. In fact, students must also pause and consider if an alternative model would have yielded a similar response.

Analyzing and assessing the model enables students to draw conclusions on the validity of their model and to reflect on how their assumptions and approximations have shaped their work and their final solution. One conclusion that the student could draw is that their model did not sufficiently answer the question posed in the original real-world problem. When students bring their work back into a contextualized setting they conclude if their approach to modelling has successfully answered the question they were assigned prior to making assumptions and approximations. You will notice in the diagram at the beginning of this chapter, that depending on the decisions made when analyzing and assessing the model, students may return to any of the previous three components. It is because of this that mathematical modelling is an iterative process which is influenced by the decisions the student makes in each component of the process.

CHAPTER **8**

Assessing Mathematical Modelling

By encountering ill-defined
problems, students see the
relevance in mathematics
and come to appreciate how
mathematics is all around them
and how mathematics can be used
to solve problems they encounter
outside of school.

What I have done in this book is demonstrate how to build capable and confident math learners who can problem solve in their everyday lives. By encountering ill-defined problems, students see the relevance in mathematics and come to appreciate how mathematics is all around them and how mathematics can be used to solve problems they encounter outside of school. To use mathematics to solve real-world problems, students need to be knowledgeable in the mathematical modelling process and be able to apply this process.

Now, shifting gears, I will provide an overview of assessment and how this can be seamlessly built into the mathematical modelling experiences of students. I will start with the types of assessment that can be applied in the classroom including formative assessment, summative assessment, and self-assessment. From this, I will provide concrete examples of assessment practices within the mathematical modelling process.

Types of Assessment

When thinking about assessment, teachers usually consider two types: summative and formative. **Summative assessment**, often called assessment *of* learning, is the assessment given at the conclusion of an instructional block, such as a unit, term, or semester to determine how well the student has learned the content. **Formative assessment**, often called assessment *for* learning, refers to opportunities to identify student learning and/or misconceptions. This type of assessment provides the teacher with an understanding of how the student is doing in relation to a concept and identifies the next steps in the learning process.

The interesting aspect of summative and formative assessments is that the same tool can be used for both. What really matters is how the student learning information is used by the teacher. The student could be given a test, asked to facilitate a presentation, work on a task, and/or share their understanding through conversation. Each of these approaches can be summative or formative. From the summative assessment perspective, the teacher would use the information gathered from the assessment to make a judgement on the learning of the student. This leads to an evaluation. From the formative assessment perspective, the teacher would use the information to gauge student learning and identify next steps.

In addition to these two types of assessment, there are opportunities for students to lead their own assessment activity. **Self-assessment**, often called assessment *as* learning, refers to students taking the time to reflect on their learning and provide a recount of what they know. Such self-assessment is based on a metacognitive approach to learning. It is important that students assess how they think and understand a concept. For a self-assessment to be purposeful, students must consider their current learning in relation to a learning target. Using a learning target allows students to identify areas of strength, weakness, and possible next steps in the learning journey.

Consider the following responses when teachers shared their perspectives of assessment with respect to mathematical modelling.

> ### PRIMARY EXAMPLE: A TEACHER EXPLAINS
>
> I had to rethink my approach to assessment. It wasn't enough to just look for whether the students could solve the problem or not. That wasn't going to cut it. I had to look for the multiple thinking points students made within their work. I couldn't just count checkmarks.

> ### ELEMENTARY EXAMPLE: A TEACHER EXPLAINS
>
> I would typically assign students a quiz and see how they did on the content. When students were engaged in mathematical modelling, I wanted a better approach to assessment, but something manageable. What I found was that I used different tools to make sense of their work.

> ### INTERMEDIATE EXAMPLE: A TEACHER EXPLAINS
>
> Assessment had to be more than just me making a decision. I needed something that would involve the students in assessment and would provide them with a chance to share their learning with me. I needed students to do some self-assessment.

The three teachers referenced the need to go beyond the traditional approach of assessment in math—looking for correct responses. Instead, the teachers identified the need to examine student thinking more closely. If teachers wanted to

It is important that students assess how they think and understand a concept.

understand how students approached, worked through, and consolidated their thinking, teachers needed a more comprehensive approach to gathering data. As the intermediate teacher shared, students should be included in the assessment process.

Consider the following responses students provided when discussing their experiences with assessing how they engaged in mathematical modelling.

PRIMARY EXAMPLE: A STUDENT EXPLAINS

My teacher talked to me about my work. Even if I couldn't get the answer, I still told her all the things I tried.

ELEMENTARY EXAMPLE: A STUDENT EXPLAINS

I liked how the teacher gave us time to share our thoughts on our work. My teacher would ask us to complete a checklist. This would show her what we thought we did right and what we needed to work on.

INTERMEDIATE EXAMPLE: A STUDENT EXPLAINS

I loved how it wasn't just right or wrong. I was given credit for the work I did and for how I was trying to solve the problem. It was about thinking instead of just getting the answers.

Students noticed how it was their thinking that was emphasized during the assessment as opposed to whether they were correct or not.

Students noticed how it was their thinking that was emphasized during the assessment as opposed to whether they were correct or not. The focus of the assessment, as shared by the three students, was on their thinking as they worked through the ill-defined problem. Each of the students recognized how the teachers were interested in what they did well and what their next steps would be.

For assessment to be effective and purposeful, there must be opportunities for all three types of assessment: summative, formative, and self. By including all three types of assessment, both the teacher and student are included in various aspects of assessment and the information gained from such an approach provides a more comprehensive perspective of student learning.

Assessment Strategies

What follows is an overview of different strategies taken in assessments. For each strategy, I will reference if it applies to summative, formative, self, or a combination.

Conversation

Assessment does not need to include paper and pencil. By having a conversation with students, the teacher can gather information on student learning. Many believe that if a student understands a concept, they can have a conversation about it. If this is true, sitting down with the student and discussing their understanding of a concept can provide the teacher with a great perspective on student learning such as their strengths, weaknesses, and any next steps required.

These conversations need to have structure since they are intended for assessment purposes. The teacher must have a clear depiction of the concept being discussed and the learning targets that the student is working toward. However, it is not a time for the teacher to simply rhyme off a series of questions that require the student to simply provide answers. That is not a conversation, that is an interview. The teacher can, however, have a collection of questions that they can ask during the conversation to steer it in a way that illuminates student understanding.

When contemplating conversation as an assessment strategy, there are aspects that the teacher must take time to consider before engaging students. These aspects include:

1. Pre-planning the conversation. It is prudent to consider the questions and prompts that the teacher may utilize when talking with their student. These questions and prompts can be both broad and specific. What is important is that the questions illuminate student learning and their understanding.
2. When will the conversations take place. The teacher should consider whether conversations will happen informally as they observe students engaged with the task, or whether they will set aside specific time for the conversation. Regardless, if the conversation occurs during the task or upon completion of the task, there is still an opportunity for the traditional flow of a conversation.
3. How will the teacher document student learning? Whether it is during the conversation or immediately following it, the teacher must decide how to record the assessment data. If the teacher can document the learning without interrupting the conversation, it can be done during the talk. If the teacher feels that it may interrupt the flow of the conversation, it may be better to record the assessment data immediately following the conversation.
4. How will the teacher monitor progress over time? If the teacher engages students in conversations over time, a decision must be made as to how data will be stored and analyzed so that future conversations can be more targeted on the student learning.

Conversations can be used as all three types of assessment. From the summative perspective, the teacher could assess student understanding of the concept as they talk. This information is used to make an evaluation of student learning. From the formative perspective, teachers could use the information to identify next steps in the student learning and create opportunities for students to engage in these next steps. From the self-assessment perspective, students can reflect on the conversation and identify areas of growth and next steps. This reflection is based on a metacognitive approach to learning.

Observation

Observing a student as they are engaged in a task provides valuable insight for the teacher.

Observing a student as they are engaged in a task provides valuable insight for the teacher. Observational assessment would involve the teacher watching from the sidelines. The teacher would not interact with the student or do anything that influences the student in making decisions. It is about observing students as they apply the concept. Through careful observation, the teacher will determine if the student is able to apply the concept and how they move toward a solution.

Observation is not simply watching. Instead, observation is detailed and purposeful. The teacher needs to have a clear understanding of the concept, identify how the concept is embedded in the students' actions that are observable, and be able to recognize whether students are making meaning. The teacher needs to have a clear understanding of what success looks and sounds like. During this observational approach to assessment, the teacher takes careful notes that detail the experience of the student.

If observation is selected as an assessment strategy, there are aspects that the teacher must consider. These aspects include:

1. Determine outcome to be observed.
2. Determine what successful completion of the outcome will look and sound like.
3. Ensure students are aware of what counts as successful completion of the outcome.
4. Identify three to four students to observe. More than this may be unmanageable for the teacher.
5. Determine a system for recording observations.
6. Be mindful that observational notes are brief and objective.
7. Date all observational notes.
8. Collect observations over a number of classes/days to get a better picture of student learning.

Observations can be used as two types of assessment: summative and formative. From the summative perspective, the teacher can use the observational data to make a judgement on student learning in relation to the learning target. This judgement then leads to an evaluation of student learning. From the formative perspective, the teacher can use the information to situate where students are at in relation to the learning target and identify next steps for the student.

Checklist

Checklists allow the assessor to hone-in on specific areas that need to be examined.

Checklists isolate aspects within a concept and/or process. From an assessor's perspective, it is either a yes or no. The assessor must decide if the student understands or does not understand the aspect of the concept and/or process. It is either a *got it* or a *not yet*.

For many concepts and/or processes, there are many aspects that coordinate to form overall understanding. This can be complex and difficult in terms of assessment. The purpose of a checklist is to provide information on student learning for the various aspects of the concept and/or process. It allows the assessor to hone-in on specific areas that need to be examined.

When implementing a checklist as an assessment strategy, there are considerations that the teacher must make. These considerations include:

1. Select descriptors that are measurable.
2. Ensure that the descriptors are clearly stated.
3. The checklist is meant to collect responses that are either yes (got it) or no (not yet).
4. Be mindful to have a checklist that does not have too many descriptors. To make this determination, consider the age of students and the outcome being examined.

5. Include a space on the checklist to record notes that would provide context to the responses.

Information gathered from the checklist can be used in the three types of assessments. From the summative perspective, the teacher can gather information to make an informed judgement and evaluation. From the formative perspective, the teacher can identify next steps in the learning journey of the student by targeting aspects that the student did not demonstrate an understanding of. From the self-assessment perspective, the student can reflect on their understanding as they complete the checklist and then identify next steps in their learning journey based on the aspects that has a no recorded in the blank.

Rating Scales

Rating scales are similar to checklists. They can isolate aspects within a concept and/or process. Concepts and/or processes can be complex and, as such, can be overwhelming to assess. To address this complexity, concepts and/or processes can be broken down into aspects and treated individually. These aspects are listed in an assessment tool whereby the assessor can select the level of understanding. This is different than with checklists. Within a checklist, the response is either a yes or no. Within a rating scale, the response fits somewhere on a scale. An example of a scale could be 0 to 5 where 0 indicates no understanding and 5 indicates comprehensive understanding. The range of numbers can be adjusted. By including a scale, more in-depth information of student learning can be gathered. Instead of having a yes or no, the assessor can be detailed in their report by indicating the level of understanding for each aspect. It can provide the assessor with an opportunity to recognize if the student is close to demonstrating understanding or if there is a significant way to go in the learning journey.

If the assessment strategy selected is a rating scale, the teacher must consider the following aspects:

1. Select criteria that are measurable.
2. Ensure that the **descriptors** are clearly stated.
3. Determine whether the indicators on the scale are numerical, visuals, or terms/phrases. This will be influenced by the age of students so that they can easily understand the **scale**.
4. Determine if the scale consists of an odd or even number. If an odd number is selected, the teacher must be fine with a neutral response given. If an even number is selected, the teacher must determine whether the student is closer to one end of the scale or the other.
5. Include a space on the rating scale to record notes that would provide context to the responses.

Information gathered from the rating scale can be used in the three assessment types. From the summative perspective, the teacher can gather information on a variety of aspects and this information can be used to make a judgement and evaluation on student learning. The information can be viewed on an aspect-by-aspect basis, a collection of aspects, or the concept and/or process as a whole. From the formative perspective, the teacher can gather information on an individual aspect, collection of aspects, or the concept and/or process as a collection of multiple aspects. This information would be used to identify next steps in the learning journey of the student. From the self-assessment perspective, the student could assess their ability to understand the various aspects within the concept and/or process. This metacognitive strategy would provide valuable information to the student to take an active stance in their learning.

Rubric

Rubrics consist of a set of criteria that are used to evaluate student learning. For each criterion, the rubric provides a scale. This scale is a level of proficiency that is often labelled as a number (one through four) or as a series of descriptors (beginning, developing, proficient, exemplary). For each criterion and subsequent descriptors, there is a concise and clear description of what performance would look like.

The intent of the rubric is to provide an understanding of the various levels of student learning for each criterion so that ambiguity is addressed. It is a more detailed approach to assessment. The assessor has a clear depiction of what student learning looks like at various points of the learning process. Having concise and clear descriptions of each criterion within a scaled approach allows the assessor and students to know the qualities and characteristics of learning that are necessary to move learning forward.

Rubrics can be an effective assessment strategy. However, there are considerations that the teacher must make. These considerations include:

1. Consider the outcome(s) that is being examined in the rubric.
2. If the outcome(s) is quite broad, there may be categories within the rubric. Each category would have its own criteria, scale, and descriptors.
3. Determine the key aspects of the outcome. These aspects become the criteria.
4. Determine if the scale consists of an odd or even number. If an odd number is selected, a neutral response may be given. If an even number is selected, a response will be closer to one end of the scale.
5. The description for each descriptor must be measurable. There must be significant differences between the descriptors along the scale.
6. The students must be made aware of the criteria, scale, and descriptors so that the learning targets are clear.

Rubrics can be used to support all three types of assessment. From the summative perspective, the teacher can gather student learning information for each criteria by identifying where students are on the scale using the concise and clear descriptions provided. This information will enable the teacher to make informed judgements and evaluations. From the formative perspective, the concise and clear descriptions within the rubric can support the teacher in identifying next steps in learning for students. From the self-assessment perspective, the student can engage in metacognition as they reflect on the criteria, scale, and descriptions. This metacognitive activity can provide students with detailed information on their learning and help them set learning goals based on next steps.

Using Assessment Data

Throughout the chapter we explored how assessment tools are flexible to support instruction and student learning in many ways. First, assessment tools are

The intent of the rubric is to provide an understanding of the various levels of student learning for each criterion so that ambiguity is addressed. It is a more detailed approach to assessment.

not necessarily tied to a specific type of assessment. The flexibility of assessment tools is rooted in the intent of the assessor. If the assessor is using the tool to make an informed judgement and evaluation of student learning, then the tool is supporting summative assessment. If the assessor is using the tool to identify next steps in the students' learning process, then the tool is supporting formative assessment. If the assessor is the student and they are using the tool for metacognitive purposes, then the tool is supporting self-assessment.

Second, assessment tools are not only helpful in single instances. It is not only about how students are doing in the present. Teachers and students can compare the information gathered from assessments over a period of time and compare and analyze progression of student learning. This comparison and analysis should use the same assessment tool and be returned to over a period of time. It can also be information gathered from different assessment tools over a period of time. By revisiting and completing an assessment tool after the initial use, the assessor can identify patterns and trends in student learning.

Teachers and students can compare the information gathered from assessments over a period of time and compare and analyze progression of student learning.

Summary

As can be seen throughout this chapter, when students are engaged in mathematical modelling there are significant opportunities to explore their learning. It is much more than counting checkmarks. This exploration can be done by the teacher and by the students themselves. Assessment, whether it is formative, summative, or a self-assessment, provides teachers and students with valuable information. For each of the assessment strategies outlined, there were options for them to be formative, summative, and/or a self-assessment.

The mathematical modelling process situates students as active learners who must construct an understanding of the problem and then decide on a possible path to a solution. When students take such a role in their learning, a significant amount of data can be collected in regards to mathematical thinking. For assessment to be meaningful and purposeful, there needs to be flexibility by the teacher to invite the complexity of mathematical modelling and the multitude of thinking points that are involved. It is about recognizing that students are engaged in thinking mathematically as opposed to doing mathematics by rote.

CHAPTER 9

Applying Mathematical Modelling Today

The teacher cannot be the busiest person in the classroom.

Think about the classrooms that you have been in as student and now as teacher. In many of these classrooms, the assumption is that the teacher is the busiest person in the room. And, for far too long, educators have accepted this as fact and have continued to allow this to happen. If our goal is to have students thinking mathematically instead of simply doing mathematics, we must shift our belief systems. The teacher cannot be the busiest person in the classroom. The teacher has already successfully completed the mathematics of the grade level they are teaching. It is now the students who should be engaged in the mathematics.

If students are the ones that should be engaged in thinking mathematically, then we should facilitate learning environments that support this belief. We must remove the teacher as the dispenser of knowledge. We must remove the need for students to get validation of their work from teachers. We have to adjust the tasks we assign students so they engage in thinking mathematically instead of applying a process by rote. We must move away from having students work on tasks that only work on a surface level. We have to dig deeper. Students should receive more than defined problems. They must be given opportunities to work through ill-defined problems as well. And we have to expand our understanding of problem solving to include the mathematical modelling process.

As referenced throughout this book, mathematical modelling is an iterative process that engages students in real-world problems. Through mathematical modelling students come to appreciate that mathematics is all around them and can be used to solve real, everyday problems.

Mathematical modelling goes beyond what students have traditionally experienced mathematics to be in the classroom. Removed are the barriers that have

Students engage in mathematics through a process that will strengthen their social-emotional learning and higher order thinking skills.

separated school from the lived experiences of students. Removed is the reliance on teachers to inform students if they have successfully solved the problem. Instead, students engage in mathematics through a process that will strengthen their social-emotional learning and higher order thinking skills.

Think about the mathematics that students have encountered in many math classrooms, from Kindergarten through Grade 8. Typically, problems start with mathematics and a context is given to apply making the problem *meaningful* for students. Unfortunately, simply providing context to a mathematical problem does not ensure *meaningfulness*. These are not culturally relevant problems. Instead, we need to assign problems that are contextualized first and where students can apply mathematics to them to determine a solution.

We want students to become capable and confident math learners. They should understand mathematics and apply it in contextualized and decontextualized situations. Encouraging this technique promotes students' autonomy where they can work through problems and use critical thinking skills to solve real-world problems they will encounter outside of school. Mathematical modelling is about making math meaningful. Mathematical modelling encourages students to be engaged in what they learn and be less passive in their learning.

When students are assigned problems that are reflective of their experiences outside of school, they see the purpose in math. Consider the following comments made by students after they engaged in the mathematical modelling.

PRIMARY EXAMPLE: A STUDENT EXPLAINS

I knew I could do it. It was hard at first, but I just kept thinking about the problem. I didn't want to give up. I can do this math.

ELEMENTARY EXAMPLE: A STUDENT EXPLAINS

It was a lot of going back and forth. I would try something and then see if it made sense. When it didn't, I would try something else. It was easy to see if my work made sense because the problem was something I could connect with.

INTERMEDIATE EXAMPLE: A STUDENT EXPLAINS

It was so much better than the problems we usually do in the math book. I actually try harder on math problems that I care about.

The comments made by each of the students demonstrate how positive mathematical modelling can be for their learning. Students are confident and capable math learners who are persistent in working through problems. They use their critical thinking skills to make sense of the problem and work through obstacles they face. Seeing purpose in solving the problems makes a difference.

Many may think there is a cost to bringing the mathematical modelling process into classrooms but take time to consider what the costs really are. The costs are that teachers move from a prescriptive, tightly controlled mathematics classroom to a classroom where student learning acts as the compass for instruction

Teachers want students to be independent, critical, flexible, creative thinkers who are able to persevere, make meaning, and clearly communicate their understanding.

and students take initiative in working through problems that are reflective of their lived experiences. I have heard from many teachers, across multiple grade levels and jurisdictions, that they want students to be independent, critical, flexible, creative thinkers who are able to persevere, make meaning, and clearly communicate their understanding. This, by definition, is what will happen when you introduce mathematical modelling to your classroom. Instead of having to create multiple problems that only go to the surface level, introduce a real-world problem that is meaningful to students and see the difference in their learning take shape. Instead of managing student learning, you facilitate student learning. You walk alongside students. What you will see is that students will accept this challenge, collaborate with others, and strengthen both their mathematical understanding and their ability to mathematically model.

Consider the following responses when teachers shared the initial thoughts of mathematical modelling in their classroom.

PRIMARY EXAMPLE: A TEACHER EXPLAINS

I was really worried about whether I would be overwhelming my students. I would be assigning problems that they wouldn't have seen before. Boy, was I wrong. Students loved it. I was actually shocked at the level of enthusiasm students displayed when working through the problem. I took on the role of facilitator in some moments and observer in others. I loved what I saw in my students.

ELEMENTARY EXAMPLE: A TEACHER EXPLAINS

I was struggling with trying to motivate my students. They were complacent and relying on me to walk them through the problem. When I assigned the problem, I thought that motivation may increase slightly, which would have been a win for me. I was wrong. Students quickly noticed how the problem was relevant to them and they took the lead. The flexibility students showed in their work and the determination they displayed was impressive. They were definitely motivated. I will certainly have students engage in mathematical modelling again.

INTERMEDIATE EXAMPLE: A TEACHER EXPLAINS

All I would see in my classroom was a sea of hands in the air. This is what I was used to. But, after going back and forth on whether to assign ill-defined problems, I started by assigning one ill-defined problem that I thought students would be interested in. Things changed that day. Instead of students relying on me for suggestions and hints, they were taking the time to understand the problem and frame it so that they could apply mathematics to it. They were independent. This is what I wanted, independence for my students.

As you can see in the above comments, the decision to bring ill-defined problems into the classroom was not an easy one for teachers. It is something that many teachers have not experienced. It is something new. However, after introducing ill-defined problems, teachers quickly saw the impact. It was a game-changer. It is not introducing more work for the teacher; it is changing the dynamics of the classroom to one where students see the value in the problem and take ownership in their learning.

If we want students to be capable and confident math learners who are not reliant on teachers, we need to step outside of what we have traditionally been doing. We need to critically reflect on our own instructional practices and consider that mathematical modelling is a natural extension of problem solving. It is the next step in terms of mathematizing student thinking.

As a student has told me when engaged in mathematical modelling, "Now I know why I need to know math!" Mathematical modelling gives mathematics a purpose and gives students a structure to address issues they encounter outside of school.

Summary

There can be hesitation in trying something new, such as the case with introducing ill-defined problems into your classroom. However, we have experienced a collective problem over time in mathematics. We have students who are *doing* math simply by following a process by rote. This is not what we want for our students. We want our students to be confident and capable math learners.

Introducing ill-defined problems into the classroom provides students with purpose and relevancy. It provides students with an opportunity to remove the barrier between their lives and mathematics in school. Through assigning ill-defined problems, students undertake the mathematical modelling process whereby they take ownership of their learning and use math to solve real-world issues. It is about having students thinking mathematically and taking an active stance in their learning.

Glossary

assumptions These are what the student brings to the ill-defined problem as a way to provide parameters and restrictions. It is about making the ill-defined problem solvable.

autonomy Being comfortable and confident in deciding on a plan and enacting it independent of support or direction from others.

blocked practice An approach where all practice questions are focused on the same concept.

checklist A list of specific learning goals that is used to record student progress. A yes or no is marked beside the specific learning goal to indicate if the student has demonstrated understanding or not.

close-ended questions Questions that have one correct response, meaning that students are either right or wrong.

cognitive processes The mental processes that are applied when working through a problem.

concrete representation When concrete materials are used to represent a mathematical concept.

contextualized This occurs when the thoughts applied to a problem are based on the information provided within the ill-defined problem.

criteria Subsets of the learning that can be measured when using a scale.

critical thinkers Those who use their knowledge and experiences to analyze and evaluate information to reach an informed conclusion.

culturally relevant A recognition of the role that students' culture and experiences play in their learning.

decontextualized This occurs when the thoughts applied to a problem are based purely on mathematics. Any context within the problem is omitted during this work.

defined problems Problems that contain the information required to reach a solution. It is the job of students to use the given information to identify an effective strategy and to arrive at the solution.

depth of knowledge This refers to how deeply a student must know, understand, and be aware of their learning so that they can reach a meaningful solution.

descriptors The qualifiers of specific measures of achievement within a scale. This can be represented using words, numbers, and/or pictures.

formative assessment An opportunity for the teacher to identify student learning and/or misconceptions. This type of assessment is meant to provide the teacher with an understanding of how the student is doing in relation to a concept and identify next steps in the learning process.

goal state The goal state is what is achieved and desired by the student. It is the preferred outcome of the problem.

ill-defined problems Problems that are missing one or more of the parameters that characterize defined problems. Ill-defined problems do not have a unique solution. What is important is that the response makes sense and that it addresses the question students encounter.

initial state The initial state is the state that students are presented with at the onset of the problem-solving process.

instructional goals The main objectives identified for a lesson, task, and/or activity.

iterative process A process that involves the student going back and forth, from a contextualized setting to a decontextualized setting. It is not intended to be linear as the student may have to return to various settings multiple times.

knowledge production The contribution to learning that students make when engaged in mathematical modelling. This learning can be assist the individual student moving forward and/or other students who have heard the thinking supporting mathematical modelling.

learning target Goals that are written in a student-friendly language that clearly articulates what students should be able to do at the end of the lesson or unit.

mathematical modelling The process by which students apply mathematics to an ill-defined, real-world problem as a way to reach a meaningful solution. Within mathematical modelling, students begin with a real-world context, identify and use mathematics to frame it, and the return to the initial context to judge the reasonableness of the response.

mathematical process The cognitive strategies that support students in acquiring and applying mathematical content.

mathematized This occurs when thinking is infused with mathematics, both in how one understands the problem and in how one approaches the solution.

meaning-making The ability to make sense of knowledge and/or experiences as they engage in a task.

modelling in mathematics This involves the representation of a mathematical concept. Students are assigned a concept and then represent it concretely, pictorially, or symbolically.

nonproductive struggle Occurs when students encounter stumbling blocks but are not able to make progress. It is through non-productive struggle that students give up on making sense of the problem and reaching a solution.

numerical representation When numbers are used to represent a mathematical concept.

obstacles An obstacle is what happens between the initial state and the goal state. Obstacles would engage students in productive struggle as students would initially be unsure as to how to move from the initial state to the goal state.

open-ended problems Problems are designed to allow for multiple solutions depending on the mathematical understanding students bring to the problem.

passive learners Do not take an active role in their learning. They rely on others to make decisions and take next steps in their learning.

points of entry This refers to there being multiple ways that students can engage with a problem, allowing for a range of strategies to be selected as the starting point.

points of exit This refers to the various responses and various ways of representing those responses which would all be considered accurate and appropriate.

problem A question and/or task is considered to be a problem when the student is presented a goal but does not immediately know how to achieve that goal.

problem posing The skill in which students can identify problems, and generate questions. Problem posing can lead to students making sense of an ill-defined problem.

problem solving A cognitive process where an immediate plan or solution is not obvious. The learner must determine an appropriate plan based on the information provided within the task.

procedural problems Problems are those where the strategy is already identified for students, and students must apply the steps accurately in order to reach the solution.

productive struggle This occurs when students are engaged in working through obstacles, but persevere. It is during this perseverance that students move closer to reaching a meaningful solution to the problem.

rating scales States individual criteria of learning and then provides a range of qualifiers to indicate proficiency within the criteria.

rich tasks The types of problems that provide students with an opportunity to make meaning within a context that is familiar to their lived experiences. Students are afforded the opportunity to select from a variety of approaches and representations as they work towards the solution, of which one or more can exist.

rote learning A situation that has resulted in a student being able to immediately recall information by memory. Students may have little to no understanding of the information they recall.

rubrics An assessment tool that identifies criteria of learning and provides a scale of qualifiers to indicate achievement for each of the criteria.

scale A range of qualifiers that highlights specific measures of achievement.

self-assessment Refers to students taking time to reflect on their learning and provide a recount of what they know. Such an assessment is based on a metacognitive approach to learning.

social-emotional learning The development of self-awareness, self-control, and interpersonal skills, and the understanding of how these skills impact learning.

strategic questioning The questioning technique used by the teacher to move student learning forward. The teacher asks specific and targeted questions, based on student responses, to assist the student in making sense of the problem.

summative assessment The assessment given at the conclusion of an instructional block, such as a unit, term, semester, to determine whether the student has achieved the content.

think aloud A strategy in which a person verbalizes the thinking they have as they engage with a given situation.

visual representation When pictures are used to represent a mathematical concept.

words-as-labels problems Problems can be thought of as simple, procedural word problems. These problems use words to provide context to a mathematical situation.

References

Anhalt, C., Staats, S., Cortez, R., & Civil, M. (2018). Mathematical Modeling and Culturally Relevant Pedagogy. In Y. J. Dori, Z. R. Mevarech, & D. R. Baker (Eds.), *Cognition, metacognition and culture in STEM education.* (pp. 307–330). New York: Springer.

Asempapa, R. S. (2015). Mathematical modeling: Essential for elementary and middle school students. *Journal of Mathematics Education, 8*(1), *16–29.*

Blum, W., & Ferri, R. B. (2009). Mathematical modelling: Can it be taught and learnt? *Journal of Mathematical Modelling and Application, 1*, 45–58.

Butler Wolf, N. (2015). *Modeling with mathematics: Authentic problem solving in middle school.* Portsmouth: Heinemann.

Byun, J. N., Kwon D. Y., & Lee, W. G. (2014). Development of ill-structured problems for elementary learners to learn by computer-based modeling tools. *International Journal of Computer Theory and Engineering, 6*(4), 292–296.

Costello, D. (2021). *Making math stick: Classroom strategies that support the long-term understanding of math concepts.* Markham: Pembroke Publishers.

English, L., Fox, J., & Watters, J. (2005). Problem posing and solving with mathematical modeling. *Teaching Children Mathematics, 12,* 156–63.

Galbraith, P. (2012). Models of modelling: Genres, purposes or perspectives. *Journal of Mathematical Modelling and Application, 1*(5), 3–16.

Greenwald, N. L. (2000). Learning from problems. *The Science Teacher, 67*(4), 28–32.

Mason, J. (2001). Modelling modelling: Where is the centre of gravity of-for-when modelling? In J. Matos, W. Blum, S. Houston, & S. Carreira (Eds.) *Modelling and mathematics education* (pp. 39–61). Chichester: Horwood Publishing, Chichester.

Ministry of Education. (2020). *The Ontario curriculum: Mathematics 2020.* Queen's Printer for Ontario.

National Council of Teachers of Mathematics. (2014). *Principles to action: Ensuring mathematical success for all.* Reston: NCTM.

Pollak, H. O. (2003). A history of the teaching of modelling. In G. Stanic & J. Kilpatrick (Eds.), *A history of school mathematics* (pp. 647–671). Reston: NCTM.

Pollak, H. O. (2007). Mathematical modelling: A conversation with Henry Pollak. In W. Blum, P. L. Galbraith, H. W. Henn, & M. Niss (Eds.), *Modelling and applications in mathematics education.* New ICMI Study Series, vol 14. (pp. 109–120). Boston: Springer.

Polya, G. (2004). *How to solve it: A new aspect of mathematical method.* Princeton: Princeton University Press.

Rohrer, D. (2009). The effects of spacing and mixing practice problems. *Journal for Research in Mathematics Education, 40*(1), 4–17.

Small, M. (2012). *Good questions: Great ways to differentiate mathematics instruction.* New York: Teachers College Press.

Small, M. (2013). *Making math meaningful to Canadian students, K-8.* Toronto: Nelson Education Ltd.

Stohlmann, M. S., & Albarracin, L. (2016). What is known about elementary grades mathematical modelling. *Educational Research International, 2016*(2), 1–9.

Van de Walle, J. A., Karp, K. S., Bay-Williams, J. M., & McGarvey, L. M. (2017). *Elementary and middle school mathematics: Teaching developmentally* (5th Canadian ed.). Upper Saddle River: Pearson Education, Inc.

Wickstrom, M. H., & Aytes, T. (2018). Elementary modeling: Connecting counting with sharing. *Teaching Children Mathematics, 24*(5), 300–307.

Recommended Resources

Boaler, J. (2016). *Mathematical mindsets: Unleashing students' potential through creative math, inspiring messages and innovative teaching*. Chappaqua: Jossey-Bass/Wiley.

Brown, P. C., Roediger, H. L. III, & McDaniel, M. A. (2014). *Make it stick: The science of successful learning*. Cambridge: The Belknap Press of Harvard University Press.

Cameron, A. (2020). *Early childhood math routines: Empowering young minds to think*. Portland: Stenhouse Publishers.

Costello, D. (2019). *Using what works: Strategies for developing a literacy-rich environment in math*. Oakville: Rubicon Publishing.

Costello, D. (2021). *Making math stick: Classroom strategies that support the long-term understanding of math concepts*. Markham: Pembroke Publishers.

Fiore, M., & Tackaberry, R. (2018). *Making sense of number, K-10: Getting to know your students so you can support the development of their mathematical understanding*. Markham: Pembroke Publishers.

Franke, M. L., Kazemi, E., & Chan Turrou, A. (2018). *Choral counting and counting collections: Transforming the PreK-5 math classroom*. Portland: Stenhouse Publishers.

Hintz, A., & Smith, A. T. (2022). *Mathematizing children's literature: Sparking connections, joy, and wonder through read-alouds and discussion*. Portland: Stenhouse Publishers.

Humphreys, C., & Parker, R. (2015). *Making number talks matter: Developing mathematical practices and deepening understanding, Grades 3-10*. Portland: Stenhouse Publishers.

Johnston Zager, T. (2017). *Becoming the math teacher you wish you'd had: Ideas and strategies from vibrant classrooms*. Portland: Stenhouse Publishers.

Kazemi, E., & Hintz, A. (2014). *Intentional talk: How to structure and lead productive mathematical discussions*. Portland: Stenhouse Publishers.

Krpan, C. M. (2017). *Teaching math with meaning: Cultivating self-efficacy through learning competencies, grades K–8*. Toronto: Pearson Canada.

Lawson, A. (2015). *What to look for: Understanding and developing student thinking in early numeracy*. Toronto: Pearson Canada.

Leinwand, S. (2009). *Accessible mathematics: Ten instructional shifts that raise student achievement*. Portsmouth: Heinemann

National Council of Teachers of Mathematics. (2014). *Principles to action: Ensuring mathematical success for all*. Reston: National Council of Teachers of Mathematics.

Pecaski McLennan, D. (2020). *Joyful math: Invitations to play and explore in the early childhood classroom*. Portland: Stenhouse Publishers.

Shumway, J. F. (2011). *Number sense routines: Building numerical literacy every day in Grades K-3*. Portland: Stenhouse Publishers.

Shumway, J. F. (2018). *Number sense routines: Building mathematical understanding every day in Grades 3-5*. Portland: Stenhouse Publishers.

Small, M. (2012). *Good questions: Great ways to differentiate mathematics instruction*. New York, NY: Teachers College Press.

Small, M. (2013). *Making math meaningful to Canadian students, K-8*. Toronto: Nelson Education.

Van de Walle, J. A., Lovin, L. H., Karp, K. S., & Bay-Williams, J. M. (2014). *Teaching student-centred mathematics: Developmentally appropriate instruction for grades pre-K-2* (2nd., Vol. 1). Upper Saddle River: Pearson Education, Inc.

Van de Walle, J. A., Lovin, L. H., Karp, K. S., & Bay-Williams, J. M. (2014). *Teaching student-centred mathematics: Developmentally appropriate instruction for grades 3-5* (2nd., Vol. 2). Upper Saddle River: Pearson Education, Inc.

Van de Walle, J. A., Lovin, L. H., Karp, K. S., & Bay-Williams, J. M. (2014). *Teaching student-centred mathematics: Developmentally appropriate instruction for grades 6-8* (2nd., Vol. 3). Upper Saddle River: Pearson Education, Inc.

West, L. (2018). *Adding talk to the equation*. Portland: Stenhouse.

Index